GO
F!GURE

TOM STANDAGE is deputy editor of *The Economist* and the author of six books, including *A History of the World in 6 Glasses*. His writing has appeared in the *New York Times*, the *Daily Telegraph*, the *Guardian* and *Wired*.

GO F!GURE

THE ECONOMIST EXPLAINS

Things you didn't know
you didn't know

Tom Standage

The Economist Books

Published in 2016 under exclusive licence from The Economist by
Profile Books Ltd
3 Holford Yard
Bevin Way
London WC1X 9HD
www.profilebooks.com

Typeset in Milo by MacGuru Ltd

Printed and bound by CPI Group (UK) Ltd, Croydon, CR0 4YY

A CIP catalogue record for this book is available from the British Library

ISBN 978 1 78125 625 1
eISBN 978 1 78283 241 6

Contents

Introduction: journey into the unknowns

DONALD RUMSFELD, US secretary of defence from 2001 to 2006, is known for many things: for being one of the cheerleaders of America's disastrous invasions of Afghanistan and Iraq; for the scandal of Abu Ghraib, the Iraqi prison where inmates were tortured and abused; and, bizarrely, for releasing an iPhone app based on Winston Churchill's fiendishly difficult variant of the game of solitaire. He is also famous for popularising the idea of "unknown unknowns". During a press conference in 2002, while answering questions about the lack of evidence that Iraq was supplying terrorist groups with weapons of mass destruction, Mr Rumsfeld said:

> *Reports that say that something hasn't happened are always interesting to me, because as we know, there are known knowns; there are things we know we know. We also know there are known unknowns; that is to say we know there are some things we do not know. But there are also unknown unknowns – the ones we don't know we don't know.*

The notion of "unknown unknowns" was not original; it is used in risk-assessment and project-management circles. But Mr Rumsfeld's use of the term introduced it to the popular lexicon. His explanation was widely mocked at the time for being gobbledegook; he was awarded the "Foot in Mouth" prize by the Plain English Campaign. This was unfair. He was making a philosophical point about the nature and limits of knowledge, building on an old saying, attributed to Socrates, that a wise man knows what he does not know. Socrates never actually put it in those words, but it is not a bad summary of his views. In Plato's *Apology* he is depicted exploring the nature of wisdom and concluding that it is dangerous to assume that being knowledgeable in one area makes you wise in others. Socrates believed, in other words, that wisdom entails understanding the limits of one's knowledge. This is called Socratic ignorance: the awareness of known unknowns, to put it in Rumsfeldian terms.

The aim of this book is to provide an entertaining assortment of both Rumsfeldian and Socratic unknowns, in the form of explanations and visualisations from *The Economist*: a selection of articles from our explainer blog, "*The Economist* explains", and graphs, maps and charts from our data blog, "Graphic detail". The Rumsfeldian unknowns are things you didn't know you didn't know: Why does Sweden have so few road deaths? How can a baby have three parents? Why do so many death-row inmates die of old age? The Socratic ones include things you've probably quietly wondered about, but have not yet got around to Googling: How do hurricanes get their names? What's the difference between Sunni and Shia Muslims? What's the difference between a dialect and a language? In keeping with *The Economist*'s comparative, global and data-driven view of the world, we also consider things some countries do differently (Why are so many adults adopted in Japan?), economic curiosities (Why are prostitutes lowering their prices?), leisure-related oddities (Why do people like pizzas in a recession?), technological teasers (How has technology made fashion week passé?) and scientific peculiarities (How do you search for time travellers?).

No doubt you will already know the answers to some of these questions. But we hope every reader will experience unanticipated lightbulb moments and enjoy unforeseen illumination. You know that mind-stretching feeling you get when you learn something new and expected? That's what we aim to deliver each week in *The Economist*, and the same is true of this book. We hope you will enjoy taking a journey, or at least a few brief excursions, into the unknowns – both known and unknown.

Tom Standage
Deputy Editor, *The Economist*
April 2016

Mind-stretchers: things you didn't know you didn't know

How a tattoo affects your job prospects

In the North Star tattoo parlour in downtown Manhattan, Brittany shows off her ink: a Banksy-inspired tableau covering both feet. Now a student at New York University, she hopes to be a lawyer one day. "That's why I got the tattoo on my feet," she says. "It's easy to hide." Once the preserve of prisoners, sailors and circus freaks, tattoos have become a benign rite of passage for many people. In America, one in five adults has one, and two in five people under 40. Women with tattoos outnumber men. But what happens when people with tattoos look for work? Alas, not everyone is as savvy as Brittany.

Although they are increasingly mainstream, tattoos still signal a certain rebelliousness that works against jobseekers, according to Andrew Timming of the University of St Andrews in Scotland. In a study published in 2013, Dr Timming and colleagues asked participants to assess job candidates based on their pictures, some of which were altered to add a neck tattoo. Inked candidates consistently ranked lower, despite being equally qualified. In a separate study Dr Timming found that many service-sector managers were squeamish about conspicuous tattoos, particularly when filling jobs that involve dealing with customers. And a survey carried out in 2011 by CareerBuilder, a careers website, found that 31% of American employers say that visible tattoos are the personal attribute most likely to discourage them from promoting someone. Some workplaces are more open-minded: a prison-services manager explained that having tattoos made it easier to bond with inmates. Firms with a younger clientele are also more tattoo-friendly. But by and large the more visible the tattoo, the more "unsavoury" a candidate was deemed to be – even if the boss had one.

Such prejudice may seem anachronistic, but it is not unfounded. Empirical studies have long linked tattoos with risk-taking behaviours such as smoking and alcohol abuse, and a higher number of sexual partners. People with inked skin are more likely to carry weapons, use illegal drugs or get arrested. The association is stronger for bigger tattoos, or when someone has several of them, says Jerome Koch, a sociologist at Texas Tech University. This may help explain the US Army's decision in 2014 to reinstate old grooming standards. These restrict the size and number of tattoos, ban ink from the neck, head and hands, and bar body art that might be seen as racist, sexist or otherwise inappropriate. The change is intended to promote discipline and professionalism. But it is making it harder to recruit to the army, says Major Tyler Stewart, who handles recruitment in Arizona. His battalion is turning away 50 tattooed people a week.

Some aspiring soldiers and other jobseekers are solving the problem by getting their ink removed. Tattoo removal has surged by 440% in the past decade, according to IBISWorld, a market-research firm. At the North Star, where Brittany's friend is getting a question-mark inked on her wrist, the prospect of such buyer's remorse seems remote. "I don't think it will help her job prospects," observes Brittany, "but hopefully it won't hurt, either." As more inked rebels turn into board members, statistics on behaviour are destined to change. In the meantime, be strategic: cover your tattoo – during job interviews, at least.

How a baby can have three parents

Roughly one baby in 6,500 is born with misfiring mitochondria, the tiny power plants found in virtually every cell that release energy from food and oxygen. That can cause a long list of problems, all of which are unpleasant, and many of which are fatal. They include diabetes, deafness, debilitating muscle weakness and progressive blindness, as well as epilepsy, liver failure and dementia. Some afflicted babies die shortly after birth. Others face a life of permanent ill-health. At the moment, such diseases are simply a tragedy that must be lived with. But doctors in Britain and America are working on a cure. If they can perfect a new technique, and if they can persuade the world's governments to legalise it, it will mark a significant moment in medical history, and not just for the benefits it will bring. For one thing, babies born via this technique would possess DNA from three people – the mother, the father and an unrelated egg donor – rather than the usual two. And it would be the first time that a genetic treatment has been licensed that affects not just the individual in question, but his or her descendants, too. How does it work?

The treatment relies on the fact that mitochondria are not just another part of a living cell. They are the distant descendants of bacteria that, a billion years ago, gave up their free-living lifestyle to form symbiotic partnerships with other cells. As a result, mitochondria possess their own tiny genomes, entirely separate from the much bigger hunk of DNA that sits inside the cell nucleus. A baby inherits its "nuclear DNA" almost equally from its mother and father. But it inherits its mitochondria only from its mother: every single one is a descendant of the mitochondria from the mother's egg cell. Although the British and American researchers are using different techniques, the basic idea is the same: to give the baby a fully working set of mitochondria donated by another woman. The scientists take an egg with damaged mitochondria, remove the nucleus (and the DNA it contains) and transplant it into a second, donor egg, whose nucleus has been removed but whose mitochondria are working normally. The result is a baby that will have nuclear DNA inherited from its mother and father in the usual way, but mitochondria inherited from the egg donor.

For some people the idea of a baby that is genetically related to three different people is viscerally unsettling (something that ethicists refer to as the "yuck factor"). Yet the Human Fertilisation and Embryology Authority (HFEA), which regulates fertility treatments in Britain, found that when it explained the procedure to a sample of the British public, most were in favour. The details of the biology may help. The amount of DNA contained within a mitochondrion, and therefore inherited from the egg donor, is minuscule: human mitochondrial DNA encodes just 37 genes, compared with more than 20,000 for the DNA in the cell nucleus. And the mitochondrial stuff is involved with only the basic, low-level functioning of the cell. So there is no chance of the children in question ending up with the egg donor's eyes, hair or personality.

That is not to say that scientists are entirely unconcerned. A report published by the HFEA in June 2014 noted that a few worries remain about technical issues, like possible incompatibilities between the donor's mitochondrial DNA and the foreign nuclear DNA with which it must interact. The fact that the modifications caused by the treatment would also be passed to the descendants of any woman born through the technique is of some concern, too. Mitochondrial replacement would thus be the first genetic treatment whose effects would travel down the generations. The HFEA recommended a few more tests to investigate such loose ends. But the scientists' main conclusion was that there is no evidence so far, including from animal trials, to suggest that the treatment would be unsafe. That is not a guarantee, of course. But, as the panel pointed out, those unknowable (and possibly non-existent) risks must be weighed against the very real suffering that would be caused by doing nothing. Britain's government, for one, seems convinced: in February 2015 it passed a law legalising the procedure. Three-parent, disease-free babies could therefore be a reality within a couple of years.

How marriage makes people healthier

The link between marriage and better health is well established. Less clear is whether marriage causes good health or vice versa; healthy people may simply be more likely to marry in the first place. A group of researchers at the Universitat Autònoma de Barcelona – Nezih Guner, Yuliya Kulikova and Joan Llull – looked at data on Americans between the ages of 20 and 64 in order to try to work out which way the causation runs. Does marriage make people healthier?

They found that the gap in self-reported health between married people and singletons persists after controlling for things like income, age and race; and that it increases over time, from three percentage points at younger ages to a peak of 12 percentage points between 55 and 59. (Cohabiting people were defined as singles in the study, but the researchers also tested what happened to the results when they were included with the married group. Answer: not much.) Next, they traced individuals' health over time, in order to isolate how much of a person's health is innate and permanent. That enabled the researchers to compensate for the fact that individuals with the physical and personality traits associated with good genes

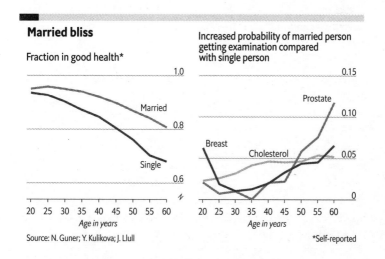

Married bliss

Fraction in good health*

Increased probability of married person getting examination compared with single person

Married

Single

Breast

Cholesterol

Prostate

Age in years

Age in years

Source: N. Guner; Y. Kulikova; J. Llull

*Self-reported

are more likely to marry in the first place. Once this is taken into account, the health gap between married people and singletons disappears at ages below 39. That suggests marriage is not having an effect on health when people are younger. Instead, the causation runs the other way: the data suggest that innate health drives up the probability of getting hitched.

But the picture is different for older people. There is still a six-percentage-point health gap between married and unmarried people between the ages of 55 and 59, a difference that cannot be explained by innate health. The researchers conclude that over time, marriage seems to be adding its very own dose of good health to a relationship, something they dub the "protective effect".

How might this effect work? Insurance is one factor, at least in America: single people there are less likely to have health insurance than couples. But another factor may be behavioural. Marriage seems to encourage healthier behaviour: a single person is 13 percentage points more likely to give up smoking if he or she gets married. Married people are more likely than unmarried ones to have preventative health checks across a range of conditions – around 6% more likely to check their cholesterol or have a prostate or breast examination at the ages of 50–54, for example. So the next time your spouse nags you to go to the doctor, give thanks. Being married is good for your health.

How to get ahead under a dictatorship

Mobutu Sese Seko, who ruled Congo for 32 years, was notorious for his "musical chairs" approach to his cabinet. His deputies were constantly shuffled around, passing unpredictably from ministerial posts to prison and exile, before once again returning to high office. Over the course of his reign Mr Mobutu burned through hundreds of ministers. High ministerial turnover is common to many dictatorships, as a study of 15 African countries shows. Why are dictators so fickle with their cabinets, and how can ministers avoid being sacked, or worse?

In a working paper for the National Bureau of Economic Research, Patrick Francois and Francesco Trebbi of the University of British Columbia and Ilia Rainer of George Mason University modelled the autocrat's dilemma of choosing which ministers he should hire to run his government. Experienced ministers are better able to help manage the country, as you would expect. But time in power also allows them to develop their own political base which, if left unchecked, could give them the means to launch a coup. Thus a dictator who wishes to avoid being overthrown must fire ministers before they accumulate enough support to topple him. In turn, ministers who manage to build their own independent support bases must decide whether they are better off remaining loyal to the current regime or attempting to overthrow it.

The time of maximum danger for ministers, it turns out, is four years into the job. In the first few years of a ministerial career they are not powerful enough to pose much of a threat. And once they have racked up lots of experience they have little incentive to rock the boat, as they would be risking a safe position for the uncertain gains from an attempted coup. But with four years under their belts they are most dangerous: just powerful enough to have a chance at the main prize, but not yet so well established as to have lost their hunger. So it is then that dictators' ministers are most likely to find themselves bundled into jail.

The authors show that those most at risk are the most senior ministers, such as those in charge of defence or finance. Those ministers' superior powers make them especially threatening. So those posts change hands a lot – ruinously for the country's economy and armed forces. The policy of firing ministers just as they begin to acquire experience on the job seriously degrades dictators' ability to govern. But for a despot who values his own survival above all else, ministerial incompetence has a lot to recommend it – something worth bearing in mind if you want to get ahead under a dictatorship.

Why India and China face a marriage crisis

China and India, home to a third of humanity, both face a marriage crisis that will last for generations. As recently as 2010, marriage patterns were normal in the two countries. Now India is revising 500-year-old laws to allow men to marry out of caste, village and state – while in China 50 million men known as *guanggun* ("bare branches") look doomed to bachelordom. What has led to this marriage squeeze?

First, millions of women have gone "missing". A generation ago, a preference for sons and the greater availability of prenatal screening meant first Chinese couples, then Indian ones, started aborting female fetuses and giving birth only to boys. At its extreme, in parts of Asia, more than 120 boys were being born for every 100 girls. The generation with distorted sex ratios at birth is now reaching marriageable age. The result is that men far outnumber women. If China had had a normal sex ratio at birth, its female population in 2010 would have been 720 million. In fact, it was only 655 million, compared with almost 705 million men and boys – 50 million surplus husbands.

Fertility rates then accentuate this distortion. When a country's fertility rate is going down (as it is in India), younger cohorts of people will tend to be smaller than older ones. If men are older than women at marriage, as they usually are, there will be fewer potential brides than husbands because women will have been born later, when fertility is lower. Then there is a queuing effect. Men who cannot find a wife right away go on looking, competing with younger men. As a result, the number of unmarried men piles up, as in a queue. By 2060, there could be more than 160 Chinese and Indian men wanting to marry for every 100 women.

This is a ferocious squeeze in countries where marriage has always been a requirement for being a full member of society. It could be hugely harmful. Almost everywhere, large numbers of single men are associated with high rates of crime and violence. No one really knows how these countries will react.

Why Sweden has so few road deaths

In 2013 the number of people killed in road accidents in Sweden was 264, a record low. Although the number of cars in use in the country and the number of miles driven have both doubled since 1970, the number of road deaths has fallen by four-fifths over the same period. Sweden's roads have become the world's safest, with only three of every 100,000 Swedes dying on the roads each year, compared with 5.5 per 100,000 across the European Union, 11.4 in America – and 40 in the Dominican Republic, which has the world's deadliest traffic. Other places such as New York City are now trying to copy its success. How has Sweden done it?

In rich countries, road deaths hit a peak in the 1970s, but have since fallen as safety measures have been introduced, both within cars themselves and on the roads they travel on. (Poor countries, by contrast, have seen an increasing death toll, as car sales have accelerated.) In 1997 the Swedish parliament wrote into law a "Vision Zero" plan, promising to eliminate road fatalities and injuries altogether. "We simply do not accept any deaths or injuries on our roads," says Hans Berg of the national transport agency. Swedes believe – and are now proving – that they can have mobility and safety at the same time.

Planning has played the biggest part in reducing accidents. Roads in Sweden are built to prioritise safety over speed or convenience. Low urban speed limits, pedestrian zones and barriers that separate cars from bicycles and oncoming traffic have helped. Building 1,500km (900 miles) of "2+1" roads – where each lane of traffic takes turns to use a middle lane for overtaking – is reckoned to have saved around 145 lives over the first decade of Vision Zero. And 12,600 safer crossings, including pedestrian bridges and zebra stripes flanked by flashing lights and protected with speed bumps, are estimated to have halved the number of pedestrian deaths over the past five years. Strict policing has also helped: less than 0.25% of drivers tested are over the alcohol limit. Road deaths of children under seven have plummeted – in 2012 only one was killed, compared with 58 in 1970.

Will the Swedes ever hit their "zero" target? Road-safety campaigners are confident that it is possible. With deaths reduced by half since 2000, they are well on their way. The next step might be to reduce human error even further, for instance by enabling cars to warn against drink-driving via built-in breathalysers. Faster implementation of new safety systems, such as warning alerts for speeding or unbuckled seatbelts, would also help. Eventually, cars seem likely to do away with drivers altogether. This may not be as far off as it sounds: several models can already drive themselves in some circumstances, such as on motorways, and self-driving cars have far fewer accidents than human-operated ones. Volvo will run a pilot programme of driverless cars in Gothenburg in 2017, in partnership with the Swedish transport ministry. Without erratic drivers, cars may finally become the safest form of transport – and Sweden will get even closer to its goal.

Constructive one-upmanship

The world is in the middle of a skyscraper boom. In 2014 a record number of tall buildings were completed; and the record for the world's tallest is being broken more regularly and more spectacularly than ever before, particularly in the Middle East. Man's skyscraper drive has, in general, been tethered to his economic one. The height of the tallest building completed in each year has tended to go up and down in tandem with the economy. On average since 1885 the yearly height record has gone up by 10ft (3m) each time. Since the 1960s the pace has picked up to 16ft.

Up until 1990, tallest buildings were almost always built in North America – in the United States or, generally during periods of economic weakness, in Canada. The years before and after the second world war saw a handful of European and South American exceptions in countries such as Russia and Brazil. But since 1990 the baton has passed from North America to China, via other Asian countries such as Malaysia and Taiwan, and the Middle East. (The title of the world's tallest building is held, for now, by the Burj Khalifa in Dubai.) That buildings are getting ever higher may please architectural buffs, but whether it makes financial sense is a different question. In terms of economic return, the ideal height for a building may not have changed much since 1930, when it was estimated (in New York) at 63 storeys. Today's buildings are heading above 170 floors.

But a paper published in 2015 by three academics at Rutgers University compared the height of the tallest building completed each year in four countries (America, Canada, China and Hong Kong) with GDP per person. They found that in all countries, GDP per person and skyscraper height were "co-integrated", a fancy way of saying that the two things track each other. In other words, developers seem to be profit-maximisers, responding rationally to rising incomes (and thus increased demand for office space) by making buildings bigger. Though ego and hubris undoubtedly afflict the skyscraper market, the authors argue that its foundations appear sound.

Skyscrapers

Height of the tallest building completed in each year
Worldwide, metres

■ North America ▨ Rest of world

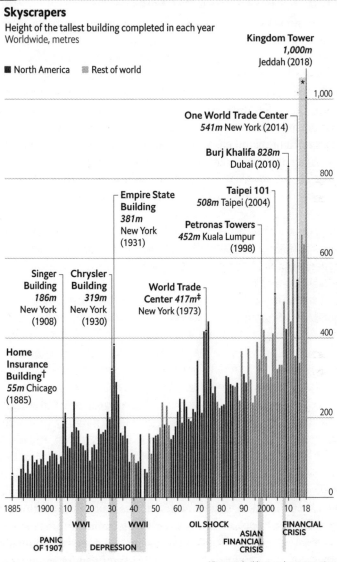

Kingdom Tower
1,000m
Jeddah (2018)

One World Trade Center
541m New York (2014)

Burj Khalifa *828m*
Dubai (2010)

Taipei 101
508m Taipei (2004)

Petronas Towers
452m Kuala Lumpur
(1998)

**Empire State
Building**
381m
New York
(1931)

**Singer
Building**
186m
New York
(1908)

**Chrysler
Building**
319m
New York
(1930)

**World Trade
Center** *417m*‡
New York (1973)

**Home
Insurance
Building**†
55m Chicago
(1885)

1,000

800

600

400

200

0

1885   1900   10   20   30   40   50   60   70   80   90   2000   10   18

WWI   WWII   OIL SHOCK   FINANCIAL
                                          CRISIS
PANIC   ASIAN
OF 1907   DEPRESSION   FINANCIAL
                                CRISIS

Sources: J Barr, B Mizrach, K Mundra & J Luo;
Council on Tall Buildings and Urban Habitat

*Forecast, buildings under construction
†Considered the world's first skyscraper
‡Not including antennae/spires

Why the first world war wasn't, really

The world – or, at least, those parts of it that participated in the original events – has recently been taking great interest in the first world war. Its almost casual beginning, between June 28th 1914, when the heir to the throne of Austria-Hungary was assassinated by a Bosnian nationalist, and the first days of August, when Germany declared war on Russia and France, drawing in their ally Britain, has fascinated historians. And the horrors that followed have fascinated everyone, though in a rather different way. But does the conflict deserve its title? It was undoubtedly a world war. But it was certainly not the first. That laurel belongs to a war that broke out 160 years earlier, in 1754, and carried on until 1763. Fighting did not start in Europe until 1756, which is why the conflict is known as the Seven Years' War in that part of the world. But it was truly global. Every inhabited continent except Australia saw fighting on its soil, and independent powers on three of those continents were active participants.

The first action of this first global conflict involved a young officer with a familiar name, who went on to greater things. On May 28th 1754, a small group of soldiers from the British colony of Virginia, under the command of George Washington, engaged a group of French troops who were interloping from New France (ie, Canada) into territory the British considered theirs. Instead of peacefully repelling them as he had been instructed, Washington ended up killing several of them, including their commanding officer. The conflict in North America then continued, with both sides fighting in alliance with local native American nations. Two years later, Britain's ally Prussia attacked the small German state of Saxony, bringing Saxony's ally Austria, and thus Austria's ally France (and therefore France's enemy and Prussia's ally, Britain), into the conflict on European soil. It is a sequence of events eerily similar to the domino effect by which an attack in 1914 by Germany's ally Austria on the small Balkan state of Serbia brought in Serbia's ally Russia, which then threatened Germany, which then declared war on both Russia and Russia's ally France.

The war rapidly globalised. Both Britain and France reinforced their colonial troops in North America, and started attacking each other's colonies in the West Indies and trading stations in Africa and India. In India, some of the princely states which had recently emerged from the dying Mughal empire also got involved, and Britain ended up taking over one of them, Bengal. The war came to South America when, near its end, Spain joined the French side and attacked one of the American colonies of Britain's ally, Portugal.

Like the first world war, this global conflict reshaped the globe. Indeed, it is the reason why the modern world is an English-speaking one. As a colonial power, France was destroyed, and did not return seriously to the business of overseas conquest until it attacked Algeria in 1830. All of North America east of the Mississippi became British, save the city of New Orleans, which became Spanish. And the foundations of British rule in India were laid as well. As for George Washington, he ended up leading a rebel army of North American colonists who decided that they would rather go it alone. The conflict he started in 1754 was the first true world war, though it is not generally referred to as such; but you can see why some historians like to call it World War Zero.

The hidden cost of Gangnam Style

Time spent watching "Gangnam Style" on YouTube*
Equivalent time to build, in 180m man-hours

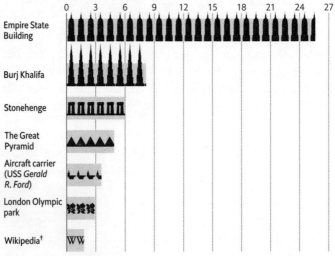

Sources: press reports; *The Economist*   *Since July 2012   †To write and edit all revisions, 2014 estimate

The loony music video "Gangnam Style" has been watched more than 2.6 billion times on YouTube, making it one of the most watched clips in history. Given the video's length (4:12 minutes) and assuming that everyone watches it all the way through, that equates to 180 million hours, or around 20,000 years. What other achievements were forgone in the time spent watching a sideways shuffle and air lasso? It took 50 million man-hours to complete the "supercarrier" USS *Gerald R. Ford*. Had people not been watching Psy – the South Korean pop star who released the song in July 2012 – they could have constructed three such ships. Alternatively they could have built five Great Pyramids of Giza, or another Wikipedia, or eight Burj Khalifas in Dubai (the world's tallest building). The opportunity cost of watching Psy's frivolity is huge. But humanity has at least been entertained.

Why the AK-47 rifle became so popular

Mikhail Kalashnikov died in December 2013, aged 94. But his 66-year-old invention, the *Avtomat Kalashnikova,* still has plenty more shots left to fire. Developed in 1947 and first used by Soviet forces in 1949, the AK-47 assault rifle and its many derivatives are now used by the armed forces of more than 80 countries, and by freelancers in many more. No one knows quite how many AK-47s are in circulation: 100 million is a reasonable guess. As a proportion of all the guns in the world – another number nobody can be quite sure about – Kalashnikovs probably account for more than 10%. Why does an ageing Soviet invention still dominate modern warfare?

The cultural impact of the AK-47 is felt all over the world. Quentin Tarantino's villains celebrate its appropriateness for "when you've absolutely, positively got to kill every [enemy combatant] in the room". Mexican outlaws boast about their *cuernos de chivo,* or "goat horns", the nickname given to the rifle because of its curved magazine. In some parts of Africa, where the gun is seen as a symbol of the ousting of colonial rulers, Kalash is a popular name for boys. Mozambique displays the gun on its flag. In Lebanon, a model nicknamed the "Bin Laden" sells for twice the price of the standard AK-47, because it is the type that al-Qaeda's former boss was seen toting in some of his videos.

The gun is nothing special. Its controls are unsophisticated; it is not even particularly accurate. But this simplicity is the basis of its success. Compared with other assault rifles, the AK-47 has generous clearance between its moving parts. That is bad for accuracy, but it means the mechanism is unlikely to jam, no matter how clogged it gets with Sudanese sand or Nicaraguan mud. Designed to be operated by Soviet soldiers wearing thick winter gloves, it is simple enough for untrained recruits (including children) to use. These features explain why the gun has remained in demand. But its success is also down to supply. The Soviet Union wanted to standardise military equipment among its allies, so it shipped giant caches of the weapons to friendly states, where it also established factories to churn out the rifles by the hundreds of thousands. (The USSR was also unconcerned with protecting intellectual property, so countless knock-offs proliferated.) The gun has now spread all over the world. But where the Soviet Union had less influence, the AK-47 was less popular. To this day, bandits in the Philippines are more likely to use variants on the M16, an American-made assault rifle supplied to the Philippine army by the United States.

With the AK-47's dominance firmly established, it has proved hard to displace. In Syria, some fighters were pictured using FAL assault rifles, which by some accounts are superior. But they didn't last long because it proved hard to find ammunition: the FAL takes 51mm-long cartridges, which are thinner on the ground in conflict zones than the 39mm-long cartridges used in the older types of AK-47, according to Nicolas Florquin of the Small Arms Survey, a Swiss research organisation. Perhaps most fundamentally, the basics of warfare haven't changed all that much since the second world war. Drones and smart weapons are revolutionising the strategies of rich-world armies. But elsewhere, much of today's bloodletting follows a similar pattern to that seen in the 1940s. Until warfare evolves, the AK-47 will remain as devastatingly useful as it was half a century ago.

Why most death-row inmates will die of old age

Gary Alvord, a Florida man who was sentenced to death for strangling three women, died in May 2013 – of natural causes. He had been on death row for nearly 40 years. The state never executed him because he was "too crazy to be killed", as the *Tampa Bay Times* put it: "In 1984, he was sent to a state hospital in Chattahoochee to be restored to competence. But doctors there refused to treat him, citing the ethical dilemma of making a patient well just so that he could be killed. He was quietly returned to death row in 1987 and remained there ever since. His final appeal expired in 1998."

Alvord's case was extreme, but condemned prisoners in America typically spend a very long time waiting to die. The appeals process can drag on for decades. It is endlessly painstaking because no one wants to see an innocent prisoner executed. Even the most enthusiastic advocates of capital punishment know that miscarriages of justice undermine their cause. For prisoners who are actually put to death, the average time that elapses between sentence and execution has risen from six years in the mid-1980s to 16.5 years now. And even that startling figure makes the process sound quicker than it is, because most condemned prisoners will never be put to death. It's simple maths.

At the end of 2011, there were 3,082 prisoners on state and federal death rows in America. That year, 43 were executed. At the current rate (which is slowing) a condemned prisoner has a one-in-72 chance of being executed each year. Because the average death row inmate was 28 when first convicted, it seems unlikely that more than a fraction of them will ever meet the executioner. In 2011, 24 condemned prisoners died of natural causes and 70 had their sentences commuted or overturned. (There were 80 fresh death sentences passed in 2011, so the number of people on death row shrank by 57.)

The number of death-row inmates who die of old age can only be expected to increase. The death penalty was restored only in 1976, so nearly everyone on death row was convicted after that date, and most were young when convicted. As they get older, more will start to die each year of heart attacks, strokes and cancer. Conditions on death row are grim; inmates age fast. They are often locked up in solitary confinement for 23 hours a day. Throughout this time, they live in fear that soon they will be strapped to a gurney and pumped full of lethal chemicals. Indeed, some lawyers argue that death row itself amounts to a cruel and unusual punishment of the sort the constitution forbids.

The seasonality and distribution of New York's dog poo

Season's greetings

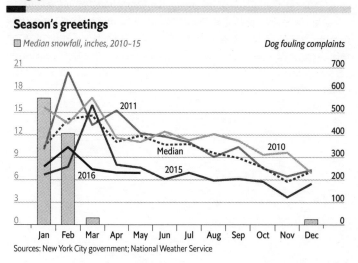

☐ *Median snowfall, inches, 2010–15*   *Dog fouling complaints*

Sources: New York City government; National Weather Service

As a global city, New York offers visitors sights they won't see anywhere else in the world. In the summer months, at the peak of the tourist season, the city also offers visitors some fairly distinct smells. As the city heats up, smells of litter and waste become especially pungent. One might, accordingly, expect complaints about dog fouling to peak in summer. Yet the opposite is true. A look through the city's "open data" programme reveals that "311" calls (that is, non-emergency calls to city authorities) about dog poo actually peak in late winter, and decline steadily over the rest of the year. In contrast, complaints of "dirty sidewalks" peak in summer, and requests to fix street lamps show no seasonality at all.

Why might this be? Some New Yorkers believe that they've found a clever loophole in pet-owner etiquette: if their pooches relieve themselves in the snow, they are somehow absolved of any responsibility to clean up after them. In winter, as snow piles up on the streets of New York, so too does the poo, buried in a heap of snow where passers-by will hardly notice the offence. Alas, the "out-of-sight, out-of-mind" method doesn't obviate the need to clean the streets – it only delays it. In March, as the snow begins to melt, the previously hidden doggy droppings reveal themselves, leaving residents barking mad – and leading to a surge in dog-fouling complaints.

Why the world's vultures are vanishing

Africa is losing its vultures. Of its 11 species of the bird, six are at risk of extinction and four are critically endangered, according to a report by BirdLife International, a nature conservation partnership. The vulture population in much of the rest of the world is at risk too. Catherine Bearder, a member of the European Parliament, has been petitioning for the European Union to save the world's vultures and eagles; the UN, too, has been discussing what action to take. Why are vultures vanishing, and why should anyone care?

Since the 1990s the population of South Asia's vulture species has collapsed by more than 99%. In 2003 scientists identified diclofenac, an anti-inflammatory drug used to treat livestock, as the main cause for this decline. Vultures eating the carcasses of animals recently treated with the drug died from severe kidney failure within weeks of ingesting it. This created two problems. The first is connected to vultures' place in the ecosystem. As their numbers declined, a host of other disease-ridden animals – in particular, rabid dogs – came to feed on the carcasses instead. Second, India's community of Parsees, who do not cremate nor bury their dead, but rather lay them out on towers known as *dokhmas* for vultures to eat, found that this tradition was imperilled. In 2006 the governments of India, Pakistan and Nepal introduced a ban on the manufacture of the drug. The number of vultures in the region has since stabilised, though they remain vulnerable.

But diclofenac remains widely available across Africa, and loopholes in European law mean it is approved for commercial sale in five European countries, including Spain and Italy, where 90% of European vultures live. In Africa, poachers use the drug deliberately to target vultures, who can reveal their whereabouts: authorities often use the presence of the birds circling in the sky as an indicator that illegally killed big game carcasses are nearby. To eliminate their winged informers and to avoid prosecution, poachers therefore lace an animal corpse with the drug. In 2013 an elephant carcass found in Namibia, Africa, was surrounded by as many as 600 dead vultures. Vultures are also endangered as a result of the demand for their body parts for use in traditional medicine in certain parts of Africa. And rapid urbanisation has disrupted vultures' natural habitats.

In October 2015, UN representatives met in Trondheim, Norway, where they agreed to add 12 species of vulture to the list of threatened species under the Convention on the Conservation of Migratory Species of Wild Animals. Iran, one of the last major strongholds for the Egyptian vulture, banned the use of diclofenac in November 2015. The European Medicines Agency confirmed in 2014 that the residues of diclofenac found in animal carcasses put vultures in the European Union at risk. As Europe awaits the Commission's decision on how best to deal with this threat, Africa would do well to take note.

Why time could be running out for leap seconds

Wonky clockwork
Change in the Earth's rotational period*, milliseconds

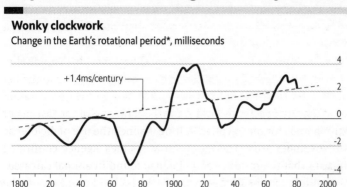

Source: Metrologia   *Compared with standard day of 86,400 seconds

At midnight on June 30th 2015, the super-accurate clocks provided by America's National Institutes of Standards and Technology (whose time-keeping can be seen by anyone at www.time.gov) did something rather odd. For precisely one second, the time they displayed was 23:59:60. That 61-second minute was not a glitch. Instead it was a leap second, an extra second inserted deliberately by the time lords of the International Earth Rotation and Reference Systems Service, designed to fractionally extend the day. It was the 26th such intervention since the world's standards bodies agreed to the idea in 1972. But now the leap second may be running out of time. Its fate was most recently discussed in November 2015 at a conference in Geneva, run by the International Telecommunications Union. Many of its member countries want the leap second abolished. But why? And why was it introduced in the first place?

Leap seconds exist to stop two different ways of time-telling from drifting too far out of sync. The first is simple, ancient and intuitive, and based on the rotation of the Earth, under which each complete rotation (or, equivalently, each of the sun's apparent trips through the sky) counts as one day. The second is new, alien and much more accurate. It uses atomic clocks to count up seconds, 86,400 of which add up to a day. The Earth's rotational speed varies over time as its hot, molten innards churn (see chart). Besides those short-term, random fluctuations, it is also slowing down, thanks to the spin-sapping orbit of the moon. That means that, over time, the two ways of telling the time lose sync with each other.

Whenever they get too far out of whack, a leap second is added to reunite them. But many people (especially the tidy-minded types who run national standards organisations) dislike the leap seconds' hackish nature. The variability of the Earth's rotation means that leap seconds must be added as and when they are required, rather than adhering to a tidy schedule. And critics argue that as the world becomes more computerised, the risks of adding leap seconds grow. Computers and leap seconds do not always mix: in 2012, the booking systems of several airlines struggled to cope with the change, as did those that run FourSquare, a social networking site.

Traditionalists retort that such worries are overblown, and point out that, despite worries about everything from internet servers to bank infrastructure, the addition of the June 2015 leap second passed without a hitch. Besides, abolishing the leap second would mean that the two forms of time-keeping begin to diverge irretrievably, although the effects (such as the sun and the atomic clocks disagreeing about whether it is noon) would not be obvious for decades at least. At the Geneva conference, the delegates were split: Australia, America and China were all in the abolitionist camp; Britain, Russia and many of its ex-Communist satellites favour the status quo. In the end they decided to delay a decision until 2023. The leap second survived, at least for the time being.

Cribsheets: things you've quietly always wondered

How a dialect differs from a language

Hong Kong's education department caused a furore in January 2014 by briefly posting on its website the claim that Cantonese was "not an official language" of Hong Kong. After an outcry, officials removed the text. But was the claim correct? The law says that "Chinese and English" are Hong Kong's official languages. Whereas some people say that Cantonese is a dialect of Chinese, others insist that it is a language in its own right. Who is right – and how do dialects differ from languages in general?

Two kinds of criteria distinguish languages from dialects. The first are social and political: in this view, "languages" are typically prestigious, official and written, whereas "dialects" are mostly spoken, unofficial and looked down upon. In a famous formulation of this view, "a language is a dialect with an army and a navy". Speakers of mere "dialects" often refer to their speech as "slang", "patois" or the like. (The Mandarin Chinese term for Cantonese, Shanghaiese and others is *fangyan,* or "place-speech".) Linguists have a different criterion: if two related kinds of speech are so close that speakers can have a conversation and understand each other, they are dialects of a single language. If comprehension is difficult to impossible, they are distinct languages. Of course, comprehensibility is not either-or, but a continuum – and it may even be asymmetrical. Nonetheless, mutual comprehensibility is the most objective basis for saying whether two kinds of speech are languages or dialects.

By the comprehensibility criterion, Cantonese is not a dialect of Chinese. Rather, it is a language, as are Shanghaiese, Mandarin and other kinds of Chinese. Although the languages are obviously related, a Mandarin speaker cannot understand Cantonese or Shanghaiese without having learned it as a foreign language (and vice versa, though most Chinese do learn Mandarin today). Most Western linguists classify them as "Sinitic languages", not "dialects of Chinese". (And some languages in China, like Uighur, are not Sinitic at all.) Objective though it may be, this criterion can annoy nationalists – and not just in China. Danes and Norwegians can converse, prompting some linguists to classify the two as dialects of a single language – though few Danes or Norwegians would agree.

In China the picture is further confused by the fact that one written form unifies Chinese-language speakers (though mainland Chinese write with a simplified version of the characters used in Hong Kong and Taiwan). But this written form is not a universal "Chinese": it is based on Mandarin. The confusion arises because many people consider written language to be the "real" language, and speech its poor cousin. The same reasoning can be used to classify Arabic as a single language, though a Moroccan and a Syrian, say, cannot easily understand each other. Ethnologue, a reference guide to the world's languages, calls Chinese and Arabic "macrolanguages", noting both their shared literature and the mutual (spoken) unintelligibility of many local varieties, which it calls languages. For the most part, linguists consider spoken language primary: speech is universal, whereas only a fraction of the world's 6,000–7,000 languages are written. Hence the linguist's common-sense definition: two people share a language if they can have a conversation without too much trouble.

Why Islam prohibits images of Muhammad

Look upwards in the magnificent place of worship in Istanbul now known as the Hagia Sophia Museum, and you will see two different ways of approaching the divine, reflecting different phases in the building's history. There are Christian mosaics, among the finest ever made, of Jesus Christ, his mother and other holy figures; and there is swirling Islamic calligraphy, which reflects the idea that God speaks to man through language, whether spoken or written, rather than through pictures or anything physical. For most of its history, Islam has had a deep aversion to the lifelike portrayal of animate beings, especially human beings, and above all to the representation of Muhammad, the messenger of God – or indeed any of the preceding prophets, such as Nuh (Noah) or Isa (Jesus). For an artist, only trying to depict the Deity could be more impious than drawing Muhammad. Why?

Such beliefs are rooted in Islam's horror of idolatry, and generally of anything that could come between man and God, or compromise the uniqueness and indivisibility of God. The Koran does not specifically condemn representative art, but it has a lot to say about paganism and idolatry; and Islam is correspondingly wary of anything that could become an idol or detract from the worship of God alone. The text most often cited in defence of the ban on representation is a *hadith*, one of the vast lore of sayings about the deeds and words of Muhammad. He is reported to have spoken harshly to a man who made his living through art. "Whoever makes a picture will be punished by Allah till he puts life in it, and he will never be able to do that." This is taken to mean that for a human, to try "making" a new being is usurping God's role – and is in any case doomed to fail.

The belief is most strongly held by the Sunnis, who form the great majority of the world's Muslims, especially the more puritanical and zealous groups such as the Wahhabis, who dominate Saudi Arabia. Shia Islam is much more open to the depiction of human beings, up to and including Muhammad himself. This difference fuels the zeal of violent Sunni groups like Islamic State, who have destroyed Shia shrines and images, claiming in doing so to be purifying their religion of idolatrous accretions. By contrast the leading figure among the Shias of Iraq, Ayatollah Sistani, has said the depiction even of Muhammad is acceptable, as long as it is done with proper reverence.

To illustrate that the ban on depiction has not been absolute, it is often pointed out that the portrayal of human figures, including Muhammad, was a central feature of Persian miniatures, under both Sunni and Shia rulers. In more modern times, the theological ban on human depiction has been challenged in many Muslim countries by the ubiquity of human images in films, on television and in political propaganda posters. In Arab countries, ingenious compromises between depiction and non-depiction are sometimes found; on road signs, for example, a headless human figure will show pedestrians where to walk. At a slightly higher theological level, it is sometimes asserted (in the course of Christian–Muslim debates, for example) that Muhammad's aversion to images had exceptions. According to one version of his life, he went into the Ka'aba – the original place of worship in Mecca – and found it full of idols, which he destroyed. But there were two images which he allowed to remain, albeit hidden from public view: those of Jesus and Mary.

How America's police became so well-armed

In May 2015, Barack Obama barred the federal government from providing some military equipment to American police departments. The extraordinary arsenal maintained by some departments – which includes body armour, powerful weapons and armoured vehicles – had become highly visible over the previous year, as a result of outbreaks of unrest in response to police violence. In August 2014 Darren Wilson, a police officer, shot and killed Michael Brown, an unarmed 18-year-old black man in Ferguson, Missouri, sparking large local demonstrations. Two days after the shooting, tactical officers – paramilitary police generally referred to as SWAT (for Special Weapons and Tactics) teams – were called in to help clear protestors from in front of Ferguson's police department. They arrived dressed for war, in riot gear and gas masks, bearing long truncheons and automatic weapons. Americans have grown used to seeing police respond to protests with tear gas, carrying automatic weapons and sniper rifles, and riding in vehicles that would not look out of place in Baghdad or Aleppo. The days of the beat cop walking the street with nothing more than a trusty old revolver seem distant indeed. How did America's police forces become so heavily armed?

As with so much else in American governance, the explanation starts with federal cash. Every year Congress passes the National Defense Authorization Act, which sets out the Defense Department's budget and expenditures. The version passed in 1990, in the wake of a sharp rise in drug-related violence, allowed the Defense Department to transfer military gear and weapons to local police departments if they were deemed "suitable for use in counter-drug activities". Between 2002 and 2011 the Department of Homeland Security, established after the attacks of September 11th 2001, disbursed more than $35 billion in grants to state and local police forces. In addition the "1033 program" allows the Defense Department to distribute surplus equipment to local police departments for use in counter-terrorism and counter-drug activities. The American Civil

Liberties Union found that the value of military equipment used by American police departments has risen from $1 million in 1990 to nearly $450 million in 2013.

And that equipment has been used. In 1980 SWAT teams across America were deployed around 3,000 times. Deployments are estimated to have risen nearly seventeen-fold since, to 50,000 a year. Tactical police units are not just common in big cities: though nearly 90% of American cities with populations above 50,000 have SWAT teams, so do more than 90% of police departments serving cities with 25,000 to 50,000 people – more than four times the level from the mid-1980s. This tremendous rise in paramilitary police forces has occurred as violent-crime levels have fallen. And while SWAT teams remain essential for high-risk and dangerous situations, most SWAT teams are deployed to serve routine drug-related warrants on private homes, often with disastrous consequences. Radley Balko, a journalist who wrote the essential book on police militarisation, has found at least 50 cases where innocent people died as a result of botched SWAT raids. Tactical teams have been deployed to break up poker games, raid bars suspected of serving under-age drinkers and arrest dozens of people for the distinctly non-life-threatening crime of "barbering without a licence". Such tactics often draw contempt from members of the armed forces. Veterans criticised police in Ferguson for intimidating the crowd rather than controlling it, for failing to share information with citizens and for escalating the standoff. One veteran noted that "we went through some pretty bad areas in Afghanistan, and we didn't have that much gear".

Americans, at last, appear to have had enough. A Reason-Rupe poll released in December 2013 found that 58% of Americans believe police militarisation has gone "too far". Politicians are finally paying attention. Rand Paul, a Republican senator from Kentucky and a contender for his party's presidential nomination in 2016, has argued that it is time to "demilitarise the police". Yet legislation has not been forthcoming. Money may have something to do with that. In June 2014, Alan Grayson, a liberal Democrat from Florida, sponsored an amendment that would have forbidden the Defense Department from transferring to local police "aircraft (including unmanned aerial vehicles), armored vehicles, grenade launchers, silencers, toxicological agents (including chemical agents, biological agents, and associated equipment), launch vehicles, guided missiles, ballistic missiles, rockets, torpedoes, bombs, mines, or nuclear weapons". It failed: not a single House leader of either party voted for it. America's defence industry donates millions of dollars to politicians, and spends even more on lobbyists. Those who opposed Mr Grayson's bill received, on average, 73% more in defence-industry donations than those who voted for it. But Mr Obama, with no more campaigns to run, faced no such constraints, and issued an executive order in an effort to stem the flow of military gear to America's police forces.

Where are the world's most "liveable" cities?

While residents of Melbourne enjoy another year in the world's most liveable city, according to the 2015 Global Liveability Ranking from the Economist Intelligence Unit, spare a thought for those who live in the 57 cities that have steadily deteriorated over the last five years.

The ranking, which considers 30 factors related to things like safety, health care, educational resources, infrastructure and environment in 140 cities, shows that since 2010 average liveability across the world has fallen by 1%, led by a 2.2% fall in the score for stability and safety. Conflicts in Syria, Ukraine and Libya have been compounded by terrorist shootings in France and Tunisia as well as civil unrest in America. In Athens, austerity rather than unrest has weighed on the provision of public services, while Kiev saw the sharpest fall relative to the 2014 rankings and is now among the ten least liveable cities in the index.

The most liveable places, notes the EIU, tend to be "mid-sized cities in wealthier countries with a relatively low population density", which explains the low ranking of near-megacities like London and New York and goes some way to explaining Melbourne's continued place in the sun.

Meanwhile, the world's ten most expensive cities are all found in Australia, Asia and Western Europe, according to the EIU's biannual cost-of-living index. Singapore retains the top spot, while weak inflation and the yen's devaluation have pushed Tokyo and Osaka to 11th and 16th place respectively. Seoul has risen from 50th place five years ago to joint ninth at the end of 2014. Asia is also home to many of the world's cheapest cities: Karachi and Bangalore are the joint cheapest locations among the 133 cities in the survey, and five of the six cheapest cities surveyed are in Pakistan and India. Caracas's descent from top ten to bottom five is due to the survey's use of an alternative exchange rate. The cost of living in New York has risen by about 23% over the past five years.

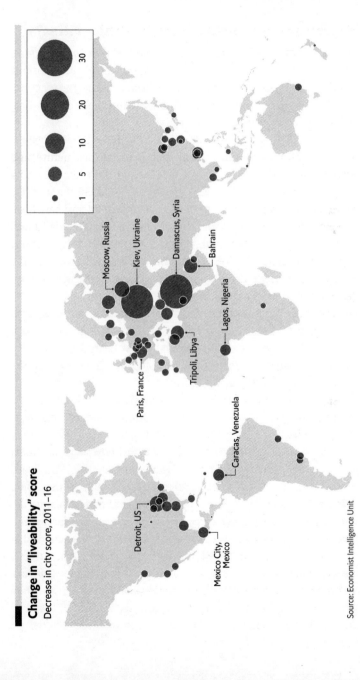

Change in "liveability" score
Decrease in city score, 2011–16

30 20 10 5 1

Moscow, Russia
Kiev, Ukraine
Damascus, Syria
Bahrain
Lagos, Nigeria
Tripoli, Libya
Paris, France
Caracas, Venezuela
Detroit, US
Mexico City, Mexico

Source: Economist Intelligence Unit

What is El Niño?

"El Niño is Spanish for...The Niño!" joked Chris Farley on a 1997 episode of *Saturday Night Live*, an American sketch-comedy programme. The skit was memorable for its absurdity but it did not do much to explain "The Niño". It aired during the devastating 1997–98 El Niño, which caused at least $35 billion in destruction and 23,000 deaths globally. The 2015–16 El Niño was even bigger, according to analysis of satellite pictures by NASA, America's space agency. So what is El Niño?

Spanish for "little boy", El Niño was so named by Peruvian fishermen in the 17th century in honour of the Christ child. They observed that every few years, around Christmas time, the Pacific grew warmer and fish vanished, migrating to cooler waters. Unlike hurricanes, El Niño is not an individual weather event: it is a climate pattern. In non-Niño years trade winds, which blow east to west, push warm equatorial water into the western Pacific, allowing cold water from the deep ocean to well up in the eastern Pacific. During a Niño, those winds slacken. The warm water that is normally pushed westward pools right across the Pacific Ocean. Water temperature increases, and heat and moisture rise into the atmosphere, altering wind and storm patterns. If ocean-surface temperatures are between 0.5 and 1°C above average during a three-month window, America's National Oceanic and Atmospheric Administration (NOAA) deems it a Niño.

A Niño generally produces heavy rains, higher temperatures and cyclones in parts of South America and east Africa. South-East Asia and Australia can see either drier weather than usual or drought. The 2015–16 Niño prompted Thailand to ration water and the Peruvian government to declare a state of emergency because of heavy rain and mudslides. It was also blamed for drought in parts of Central America, Indonesia, the Philippines and Australia. The Panama Canal's water levels fell so far that officials there limited traffic. Globally, the effects can be devastating, as agricultural and economic havoc fuel political conflict. Indeed, Columbia University's Earth Institute found that a Niño doubles the risk of civil wars across 90 tropical countries. Yet not all its effects are bad. One study shows that a Niño may reduce the number of tornadoes in the Midwest. It may also suppress hurricanes from forming in the Atlantic Ocean, and lead to milder winters in America's Northeast.

Some scientists like to use headline-grabbing language, such as "Godzilla El Niño" and "Bruce Lee El Niño", to indicate how powerful its effects can be. A powerful Niño could also affect the climate-change debate. A Niño's rapid release of stored heat produces sudden global warming. It is, many climatologists believe, no coincidence that a recent apparent pause in global warming coincides with the quiet period since the last big Niño. Godzilla El Niño, by contrast, may have helped make 2015 the hottest year on record, by a long shot.

Grid of grievances

On April 2nd 2015, Iran and six world powers (America, Russia, China, Britain, France and Germany) agreed the outline of a deal to restrict Iran's ability to develop a nuclear bomb for a decade, in return for a gradual easing of sanctions. President Barack Obama said the deal promised to resolve by diplomatic means one of the greatest threats to world security. But it remains unclear how the accord will affect the turmoil in the Middle East. Four Arab civil wars are under way – in Iraq, Syria, Libya and Yemen – with Iran,

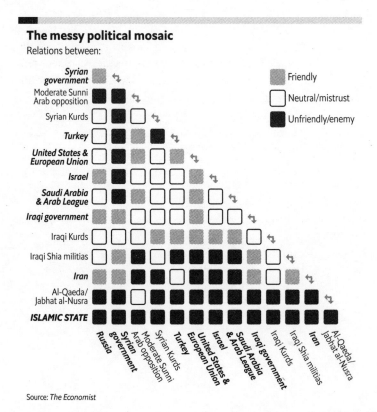

The messy political mosaic

Relations between:

Friendly
Neutral/mistrust
Unfriendly/enemy

Syrian government · Moderate Sunni Arab opposition · Syrian Kurds · Turkey · United States & European Union · Israel · Saudi Arabia & Arab League · Iraqi government · Iraqi Kurds · Iraqi Shia militias · Iran · Al-Qaeda/Jabhat al-Nusra · ISLAMIC STATE

Source: *The Economist*

America and Saudi Arabia supporting a complex mix of warring parties, as our chart shows.

The conflicts reflect multiple divisions over religion, ideology, ethnicity and class. But the sectarian rift – in which Iran supports Shias and their allies, while Saudi Arabia backs at least some of the Sunnis – has become more acute. It is most apparent in Iraq, where the government is dominated by Shias and is allied to Iran. Most Sunni areas have been taken over by jihadists of the so-called Islamic State, who also control swathes of eastern Syria. In Syria President Bashar Assad's Alawite minority sect, regarded as an offshoot of Shia Islam, dominates the government and is propped up by Iran and its Lebanese proxy, Hizbullah. The rebels are mostly Sunni and fragmented. In Yemen the link between the Houthis (followers of the Zaydi branch of Shia Islam) and Iran (devotees of the Twelver branch) is perhaps least clear. Yet this is where Saudi Arabia and other Sunni countries have decided to draw a red line against Iranian encroachment: the Saudis lead a ten-nation coalition involved in bombing the Houthis.

America, for its part, straddles the divide. In Iraq it operates alongside Iran to support the Baghdad government; in Syria it gives lukewarm support to some of the more moderate rebels; in Yemen it is providing intelligence and logistical help to the Saudi military operation. Where there is no Shia–Sunni divide, there are marked Sunni–Sunni splits. In Egypt the government of Abdel-Fattah al-Sisi is supported by Saudi Arabia and the United Arab Emirates against the Muslim Brotherhood, which is backed by Turkey and Qatar. The same two groupings support rival governments in Libya.

The difference between "less" and "fewer"

Many people insist on a bright-line distinction between "fewer" and "less", and get quite agitated by the subject. David Foster Wallace's novel *Infinite Jest* featured the Militant Grammarians of Massachusetts, who boycott stores with signs reading "12 items or less". A few vigilantes have defaced such signs in real life. What is the distinction, and why does it matter?

Nouns can be "count nouns" or "mass nouns". Count nouns are usually distinct things that can be counted, and take a plural: think "houses" or "shirts". Mass nouns can't usually be counted or made plural: think "water" or "oatmeal". (They can sometimes be counted, as in a fancy restaurant offering several different waters, but "water" in ordinary use is otherwise a mass noun.) Under the traditional rule, "fewer" goes with count nouns and "less" with mass nouns. Hence "My sister has fewer shirts than I do", but "My brother has less oatmeal than I do". The rule was first proposed in this form in 1770 by Robert Baker in *Reflections on the English Language*.

But Baker expressed this as a preference, not a rule, perhaps because there are many shadings on it. The mass-count distinction does not always line up with the real-life properties of things: "clothing" is a mass noun (so it's "less clothing") but "clothes" is a count noun (so "fewer clothes"). Clothes are discrete items – like a typical count noun. And yet you can't count them: "he is wearing four clothes" makes no sense. Meanwhile, some count nouns don't represent discrete things at all. Take time and distance: years and miles are count nouns, but they represent arbitrary sections on a continuum. This probably is why many people find "I've lived here less than three years" more natural than "I've lived here fewer than three years". And "less" is almost always more natural than "fewer" after one, in sentences like "that's one less thing to deal with".

Finally, there is the question of style. "Fewer" is never used with mass nouns, but in casual speech, "less" is often used with count nouns. "She won't go out with anyone with less than three cars" is fine for the barstool, but using this phrasing in print is likely to attract an editorial correction. The so-called rule has never reflected reality: as far back as the ninth century we find Alfred the Great writing *swa mid laes worda, swa mid ma* ("be it with less words or with more"). Even so, it is a good guideline for formal writing – and good for keeping the Militant Grammarians of Massachusetts out of your supermarket.

Who wants to live for ever?

Over the past 100 years, mankind has made great leaps in eliminating diseases and learning how to keep people alive. The life expectancy of a person born in the US in 1900 was just 47 years. Eighty years later that figure had increased to 70 years for men and 77 years for women. But since then progress has slowed: a boy born in America in 2013 is expected to live just six years longer than one born in 1990. And not all his twilight years will be golden.

Statisticians at the Institute for Health Metrics and Evaluation at the University of Washington have calculated figures that adjust life expectancy at birth for the number of healthy years that a person can be expected to enjoy, free from disease and disability. An American male born in 1990 is expected to live until 72, but can expect nine years of ill health. By 2013, life expectancy increased to 76 years, but with ten and a half years living in ill health. Since 1990, American men have gained an additional three years of healthy life and an additional four and half years of ill health. Such has been the slow rate of longevity progress in America, that Chinese and Iranian men born today are expected to live longer and healthier lives than their American counterparts. The most impressive increase in healthy life expectancy was found in Iran: between 1990 and 2013 it increased by around nine years for women and eleven for men. India and China also did well on this score: in both countries, women can expect another eight years of life in good health, and men can expect six.

America spends a great deal of money keeping people alive for longer: around one quarter of America's spending on Medicare, or health care for the elderly, is spent during the last six months of life alone. Perhaps knowing when to give up the ghost is the key to real happiness and national wealth.

Life expectancy at birth
Years (selected countries ranked by average healthy life expectancy in 2013)

In 1990
■ Healthy life expectancy
■ Additional years of ill health*

1990–2013
□ Increase in healthy life expectancy
▨ Increase in additional years of ill health

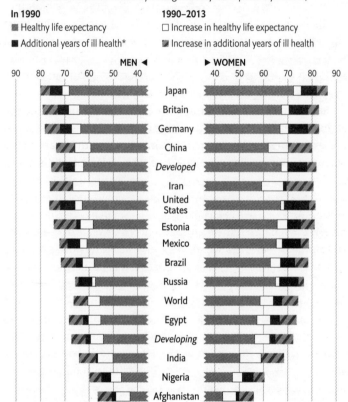

Source: "Global, regional, and national disability-adjusted life years…", by Christopher Murray *et al, The Lancet*, 2015

*Where figure is not shown, life expectancy in 1990 is less than healthy life expectancy in 2013

Why so many Koreans are called Kim

A South Korean saying claims that a stone thrown from the top of Mount Namsan, in the centre of the capital Seoul, is bound to hit a person with the surname Kim or Lee. One in every five South Koreans is a Kim – in a population of just over 50 million. And from the current president, Park Geun-hye, to rapper Psy (born Park Jae-sang), almost one in ten is a Park. Taken together, these three surnames account for almost half of the population of South Korea today. Neighbouring China has around 100 surnames in common usage; Japan may have as many as 280,000 distinct family names. Why is there so little diversity in Korean surnames?

Korea's long feudal tradition offers part of the answer. As in many other parts of the world, surnames were a rarity until the late Joseon dynasty (1392–1910). They remained the privilege of royalty and a few aristocrats (*yangban*). Slaves and outcasts such as butchers, shamans and prostitutes, but also artisans, traders and monks, did not have the luxury of a family name. As the local gentry grew in importance, however, Wang Geon, the founding king of the Goryeo dynasty (918–1392), tried to mollify it by granting surnames as a way to distinguish faithful subjects and government officials. The *gwageo*, a civil-service examination that became an avenue for social advancement and royal preferment, required all those who sat it to register a surname. Thus elite households adopted one. It became increasingly common for successful merchants to take on a last name, too. They could purchase an elite genealogy by physically buying a genealogical book (*jokbo*) – perhaps that of a bankrupt *yangban* – and using his surname. By the late 18th century, forgery of such records was rampant. Many families fiddled with theirs: when, for example, a bloodline came to an end, a non-relative could be written into a genealogical book in return for payment. The stranger, in turn, acquired a noble surname.

Because family names such as Lee and Kim were among those used by royalty in ancient Korea, they were preferred by provincial elites and, later, by commoners when plumping for a last name. This small pool of names originated from China, adopted by the Korean court and its nobility in the seventh century in emulation of noble-sounding Chinese surnames. (Many Korean surnames are formed from a single Chinese character.) So to distinguish one's lineage from those of others with the same surname, the place of origin of a given clan (*bongwan*) was often tagged onto the name. Kims have around 300 distinct regional origins, such as the Gyeongju Kim and Gimhae Kim clans, though the origin often goes unidentified except on official documents. The limited pot of names meant that no one was quite sure who was a blood relation; so, in the late Joseon period, the king enforced a ban on marriages between people with identical *bongwan* (a restriction that was lifted only in 1997). In 1894 the abolition of Korea's class-based system allowed commoners to adopt a surname too: those on lower social rungs often adopted the name of their master or landlord, or simply took one in common usage. In 1909 a new census-registration law was passed, requiring all Koreans to register a surname.

Today clan origins, once deemed an important marker of a person's heritage and status, no longer bear the same relevance to Koreans. Yet the number of new Park, Kim and Lee clans is in fact growing: more foreign nationals, including Chinese, Vietnamese and Filipinos, are becoming naturalised Korean citizens, and their most popular picks for a local surname are Kim, Lee, Park and Choi, according to government figures. Hence, for example, the Mongol Kim clan, or the Taeguk (of Thailand) Park clan. As a result, the popularity of these three names seems likely to continue.

Why you can't get a signal on your phone

Mobile phones have advanced in leaps and bounds over the past few years. What was once a simple portable telephone and text-messaging device is now typically a powerful internet-access terminal, a high-quality digital camera, a portable games console, a music-player and a high-definition TV you can watch anywhere. But as handsets have become more capable, powerful and ubiquitous, networks do not seem to have kept up. Sometimes all you want to do is make a call or send a quick e-mail, but you can't get a signal in some corners of your home or office. Venture out of town and you may not be able to get a signal at all – or, if you can, it's only a slowpoke 2G connection. Why have wireless networks lagged behind progress in handsets?

Part of the explanation is technical. Signals sent over voice-centric 2G networks generally propagate further and provide better in-building coverage than those of data-centric 3G networks. That is because 2G signals typically use the 900MHz and 1800MHz frequency bands, whereas in most countries 3G signals are generally sent in the 2100MHz band. Signals sent at higher frequencies don't travel so far or penetrate walls so well. This isn't entirely a bad thing, in one sense: the shorter range of 3G signals means that networks can be built using a larger number of smaller cells, which boosts overall capacity. But unless you are close to a 3G base-station, you'll only get a 2G signal. 3G networks do better on speed and capacity, but can be worse on coverage.

There are also economic reasons. People tend to upgrade their handsets every year or two, so the turnover of new devices is very rapid and new features are adopted quickly. Upgrading a network, by contrast, is a hugely expensive process that takes years and costs billions of dollars, as new sites are acquired, base-stations and antennas are erected and backhaul connections are installed to connect them to the network. Given the expense, operators add capacity where it is most needed and will benefit the most people. In practice that means city centres and transport hubs, then major roads, tend to get upgraded first, followed by suburban areas. Rural areas may never get any more than patchy coverage, let alone whizzy network upgrades, because the density of users isn't great enough to justify the expense. To put it more cynically, network operators have an incentive to build the worst network they can get away with.

The good news is that things are improving on a number of fronts. In many countries, the low-frequency 2G spectrum is being "refarmed" (ie, repurposed) for 3G, which allows 3G signals to travel further. Newer 4G networks operate in a range of frequency bands, using 700MHz and 800MHz signals in many countries to provide wider coverage. (That also helps explain why you can get 4G in places where you couldn't get 3G.) And additional low-band spectrum is being made available in some countries, for example through an auction of a 600MHz spectrum in America. Finally, small base-stations called picocells and femtocells, which provide in-building cellular coverage, are becoming increasingly widespread in shopping malls, offices and railway stations, along with Wi-Fi. But just as you can never be too rich or too thin, you can never have fast enough wireless coverage – so smartphone users will always want more.

How hurricanes get their names

On October 29th 2012, Hurricane Sandy hit New York. Some 200 people died and the costs were put at $71 billion, a toll that has been surpassed only by the fury of Hurricane Katrina, which struck New Orleans in 2005. But neither Sandy nor Katrina will ever strike again: meteorologists promptly retired both names. The United Nations' World Meteorological Organisation chooses storm names from lists that are recycled every six years, but discards those that have been attached to storms of dreadful destruction. Controversial ones like Adolf and Isis have also been struck off. So how are hurricanes named – and how did this convention come about?

For several hundred years, Caribbean islanders, who seemed to face the wrath of God with great frequency, named hurricanes after saints. But storm-naming was haphazard. In the 1850s an Atlantic storm that wrecked a boat named *Antje* became "Antje's hurricane", while another that hit Florida on Labor Day took the name, "Labor Day". At the end of the 19th century, Clement Wragge, an Australian forecaster, tried to impose a system, naming storms after letters of the Greek alphabet. When the Australian government refused to recognise this, he began naming hurricanes after politicians instead. Unsurprisingly, a system that appeared to describe a politician as "causing great distress" or "wandering aimlessly about the Pacific" encountered resistance. Another approach was to describe hurricanes by the latitude and longitude co-ordinates that had enabled meteorologists to track them. But this was unhelpful to those who lived on the coast and relied on succinct life-saving counsel over the radio.

Today's official practice of naming hurricanes began in 1950, when storms were called after phonetic alphabets then used by American servicemen (Able, Baker, Charlie). These names were short and tripped lightly off tongues and keyboards. Exchanging notes among thousands of scattered radio stations, ships at sea and coastal bases became easier. The new technique proved particularly useful when two storms of varying ferocity occurred at the same time. However, only two years later, in 1952, a new international phonetic alphabet was adopted (Alpha, Bravo, Charlie, and so on) causing some confusion. So, following the naval meteorologists who named storms after their wives, the American National Hurricane Center began using female names. The practice proved popular – and controversial. The media delighted in describing "tempestuous" female hurricanes, "teasing" and "flirting" with coastlines. Women's-rights activists campaigned against the practice, and ever since 1978, storm names have alternated between the sexes.

Such names matter more than one might expect. In 2014 a study by researchers at Arizona State University and the University of Illinois found that hurricanes with feminine names killed more people than those with masculine ones. This has little to do with their ferocity, which was randomly distributed, but rather with people's reactions to them. It seems that tropical storms with women's names are taken less seriously than those with male names.

How people in different countries spend their money

Spending in different countries seems to reflect national stereotypes, according to household expenditure data compiled by Eurostat. Russians splash 8% of their money on booze and cigarettes – far more than most developed countries – while fun-loving Australians spend a tenth of their cash on recreation, and bookish South Koreans splurge more than most on education. Some differences can be attributed to variations in the level of economic development. Richer places like the US and Australia, where household expenditure is around $30,000 per person, will tend to spend a smaller share of their costs on food than Mexico and Russia, where average spending is around $6,000. Political differences play a part too. In America, where health-care provision is predominantly private, it eats up over a fifth of each household's budget; in the European Union, where public health care is common, households spend only 4% on it. In Russia, government-subsidised housing and heating make living cheaper, and this means money is left over for the finer things in life.

Aggregating European Union countries hides interesting regional differences in spending, however. In Malta, an island nation of 450,000 south of Italy, almost 20% of household expenditure goes on restaurants or hotels. In Lithuania that figure is 2.9%. Relative to much of the EU, Lithuania is a poor country with a per capita household expenditure of $8,500, half the EU average. Its people spend a larger share of their budget on food and clothing than any other EU country. The fun-loving Dutch spend most on recreation, while Greeks spend the least – a trait that pre-dates the financial crisis. Perhaps they are paying down debt instead?

How they spend it

Household spending*, % of total, 2013 or latest, includes taxes

Within category ● highest spend ● above average ● below average ○ lowest spend

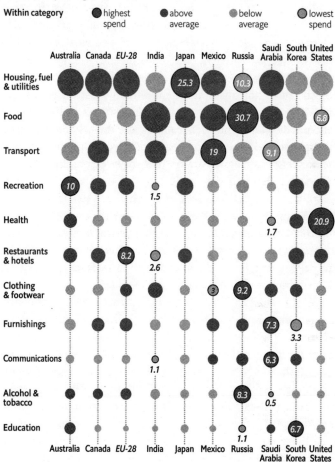

	Australia	Canada	EU-28	India	Japan	Mexico	Russia	Saudi Arabia	South Korea	United States
Housing, fuel & utilities					25.3		10.3			
Food							30.7			6.8
Transport						19		9.1		
Recreation	10			1.5						
Health								1.7		20.9
Restaurants & hotels			8.2	2.6						
Clothing & footwear						3	9.2			
Furnishings								7.3	3.3	
Communications				1.1				6.3		
Alcohol & tobacco							8.3	0.5		
Education							1.1		6.7	

Source: Eurostat

*Categories exclude miscellaneous spending

What defines a "frozen conflict"?

Wars are defined by their winners and losers. But some conflicts seem to last for decades without yielding a clear result. These are called "frozen conflicts", and several of them exist today, mainly in Eurasia. What defines a frozen conflict, and what makes these disputes so intractable?

First, it needs the support of a large power with the funds and the willingness to sustain the dispute. Russia is good at this. Ever since the break-up of the Soviet Union, Moscow has taken sides in a number of spats in the Caucasus region. It has backed rebels in South Ossetia and Abkhazia since the early 1990s – two regions that are part of Georgia. In 2008, Moscow even sent in tanks to support South Ossetian separatists.

Second, the supporting power usually has a financial or strategic interest in the contested area over which it wishes to exert influence. Ukraine, a country largely dependent on Russian gas imports, is a prime example. Ukraine and Russia have political and cultural connections, and companies in the industrialised east of Ukraine, such as Antonov, an aircraft manufacturer, are important suppliers to Russia's armed forces and its heavy industry. So Russia is reluctant to let Ukraine slip out of its sphere of influence, and perpetuates the frozen conflict in Ukraine's east.

Frozen conflicts can thaw, escalating into full-scale shooting wars at short notice. In Nagorno-Karabakh, a region between Armenia and Azerbaijan, soldiers on both sides still exchange fire, even though a ceasefire was signed in 1994. If frozen conflicts prove hard to resolve, it is generally because powerful interests like it that way.

How Shia and Sunni Muslims differ

Clashes between Islam's two big sects, the Sunni and the Shia, take place across the Muslim world. In the Middle East a potent mix of religion and politics has sharpened the divide between Iran's Shia government and the Gulf states, which have Sunni governments. A report by the Pew Research Centre, a think-tank, found that 40% of Sunnis do not consider Shia to be proper Muslims. So what exactly divides Sunni and Shia Islam, and how deep does the rift go?

The argument dates back to the death in 632 of Islam's founder, the Prophet Muhammad. Tribal Arabs who followed him disagreed over who should succeed him, and inherit what was both a political and a religious office. The majority, who went on to become known as the Sunnis, and today make up 80% of Muslims, backed Abu Bakr, a friend of the Prophet and father of his wife, Aisha. Others considered Muhammad's kin the rightful successors. They claimed the Prophet had anointed Ali, his cousin and son-in-law – and became known as the Shia, a contraction of "shiaat Ali", the partisans of Ali. Abu Bakr's backers won out, though Ali did briefly rule as the fourth caliph, the title given to Muhammad's successors. Islam's split was cemented when Ali's son Hussein was killed in 680 in Karbala (modern Iraq) by the ruling Sunni caliph's troops. Sunni rulers continued to monopolise political power, while the Shia lived in the shadow of the state, looking instead to their imams, the first twelve of whom were descended directly from Ali, for guidance. As time went on the religious beliefs of the two groups started to diverge.

Today the world's 1.6 billion Muslims all agree that Allah is the only God and Muhammad his messenger. They follow the five ritualistic pillars of Islam, including Ramadan, the month of fasting, and share a holy book, the Koran. But while Sunnis rely heavily on the practice of the Prophet and his teachings (the "sunna"), the Shia see their ayatollahs as reflections of God on Earth. This has led Sunnis to accuse the Shia of heresy; for their part, the Shia point out that Sunni dogmatism has given rise to extremist sects such as the puritanical Wahhabis. Most Shia sects place importance on the belief that the twelfth and final imam is hidden (or "in occultation") and will reappear one day to fulfil Allah's divine will. Meanwhile, their sense of marginalisation and oppression has led to mourning ceremonies such as ashura, in which followers flagellate themselves to commemorate Hussein's death at Karbala.

There has never been a clash between the Shia and Sunni on the scale of the Thirty Years War, which saw Christian sects fight each other in 17th-century Europe with great loss of life. This is partly because the Shias, ever mindful of their minority status, retreated. The lines that divide Muslims in the Middle East today depend on politics as much as religion. The revolutions in the region have pitted Shia governments against Sunni Gulf states such as Saudi Arabia and Qatar, who have supported their co-religionists with cash. This is strengthening Sunni assertiveness and making the Shia feel more threatened than usual. In most cases, though, members of the two sects still live harmoniously together.

Which government asks for the most data from Facebook?

Whose data?
Government requests* to **facebook** for user-account data

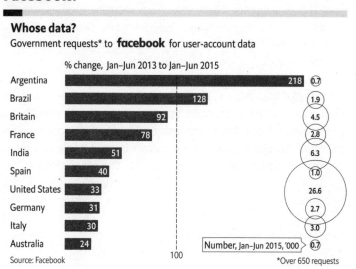

% change, Jan–Jun 2013 to Jan–Jun 2015

Country	% change	Number, Jan–Jun 2015, '000
Argentina	218	0.7
Brazil	128	1.9
Britain	92	4.5
France	78	2.8
India	51	6.3
Spain	40	1.0
United States	33	26.6
Germany	31	2.7
Italy	30	3.0
Australia	24	0.7

Source: Facebook   100   *Over 650 requests

Facebook issues regular reports on the number of requests it receives from governments around the world for data about its users' accounts. Its report for the first half of 2015 shows the demand for such information is rising. Requests in the United States have jumped by a third since the first report, in 2013. Britain, in third place for total requests, saw an increase of 92% over the same period. Although the absolute numbers are small (the US made 26,600 requests, or 16 for every 100,000 Facebook users in the country), governments increasingly regard such material as a useful resource. Other social-media firms, including Twitter and Snapchat, have also noted a rise in government requests. Although companies say they push back hard to protect users' online privacy wherever possible, they are obliged to accede to legal requests. In July 2015, Facebook lost a case in New York where it contested 381 search-warrant requests, mostly on the grounds that legally only a defendant can contest a search warrant. Europe and America, meanwhile, have been bickering over "safe harbour" rules that govern how American firms treat information about European citizens. People's personal data may be up in the cloud, but the question of who has the right to access it is up in the air.

The difference between comets, asteroids and meteors

There's much more to the solar system than the sun and its retinue of planets. There are comets, one of which, 67P/Churyumov–Gerasimenko, resembles a rubber duck, and has been inspected in detail by the *Rosetta* space probe. *Dawn*, another space probe, visited an asteroid called Vesta, before heading off to another asteroid called Ceres. Throughout the year observers on Earth may witness showers of meteors. And sometimes fireballs appear in the sky, like that seen over Chelyabinsk in Russia in 2013. So what's the difference between a comet, an asteroid and a meteor, and what is the relationship between them?

Start with comets. They formed billions of years ago around the far fringes of the solar system, and consist of lumps of ice mixed with rock, dust and frozen gases. As a comet's orbit brings it closer to the sun, it heats up and grows a "tail" of water and dust. Asteroids, by contrast, formed closer to the sun: they are leftovers from the era of planetary formation, and are mostly found within the orbit of Jupiter. Rocky in nature, they are also sometimes called planetoids or minor planets. Despite their name (*aster* means "star" in Latin), they have nothing to do with stars.

Asteroids smaller than a few metres across are known as meteoroids, as are the small pieces of dust, rock and ice shed by comets. When a meteoroid enters the Earth's atmosphere it appears as a meteor or shooting star to observers – or, if it is large enough, as a fireball. If any of it survives re-entry and reaches the ground, the resulting pieces are called meteorites.

Meteor showers occur when the Earth passes across the trail of debris left behind by a comet. Because the orbits of comets are known, the positions of these trails can be predicted, and thus the dates of meteor showers: the Geminids in mid-December, for example, and the Perseids in mid-August. In short: comets are big and icy, asteroids are big and rocky, and meteors are small bits of debris burning up in the Earth's atmosphere in a final blaze of glory. Happy skywatching.

What Satanists actually believe

In November 2012, a stone monument inscribed with the Ten Commandments was placed on the grounds of Oklahoma's state capitol. Seven years earlier, in a case called *Van Orden v Perry*, the United States Supreme Court had ruled that a Ten Commandments monument placed on the Texas state capitol grounds did not violate the First Amendment's clause forbidding government from making any law "respecting the establishment of religion". But if that ruling allows Christian monuments, it ought to allow others, too. Accordingly, in December 2013 the Satanic Temple launched a campaign to place a monument of its own next to the Ten Commandments, reasoning that it would give Oklahomans "the opportunity to show that they espouse the basic freedoms spelled out in the Constitution". The Satanists duly unveiled their monument's proposed design: a winged creature with the torso of a man, the head of a goat and horns sits on a throne beneath a Pentagram, two fingers sagely raised as two children look on in wonder. America's Satanists, it seems, have a sense of humour. But what do they actually believe?

That turns out to be a difficult question to answer. Perhaps unsurprisingly, Satanists are a rather fractious bunch, with many different organisations, beliefs and rituals. Many of these organisations are wholly or partly occult, with much hidden from non-adherents. Some are spiritualists: they worship Satan as a deity. Adherents of the Joy of Satan Ministries, for instance, "know Satan/Lucifer as a real being", and believe he is "the True Father and Creator God of humanity". Others – notably the Church of Satan, founded by Anton LaVey, the most renowned occultist since Aleister Crowley; and the Satanic Temple – are materialist, and reject belief in supernatural beings. Lucien Greaves, a spokesman for the Satanic Temple, describes himself as "an atheist when it comes to supernatural beliefs", and says that for him Satanism stands for "individual sovereignty in the face of tyranny, and the pursuit of knowledge even when that knowledge is dangerous".

LaVey's "Satanic Bible" proclaims "Life is the great indulgence – death the great abstinence! Therefore make the most of the HERE AND NOW! ... Choose ye this day, this hour, for no redeemer liveth!"

Despite these differences, certain commonalities link many spiritual and materialist branches of Satanism: namely a belief that the worship of a supernatural deity – and the ecclesiastical structure that evolved to support such worship – places needless restrictions on human knowledge and progress; and a belief in science, rationality and learning, without restrictions. Peter Gilmore, LaVey's successor as head of the Church of Satan, distinguishes between "carnal people and spiritual people": he believes the latter need a "spooky daddy in the sky", whereas he is "happy being the center of [his] universe". In this sense, materialist Satanism seems close to, if not indistinguishable from, organised atheism, or perhaps atheism with rituals. But Mr Gilmore says his church uses Satan in the original Hebrew sense as "The Adversary" – "a figure who will stand up and challenge". Satan in this sense becomes a sort of literary figure or metonymy for challenging orthodoxy, rather than an evil or bloodthirsty god.

All of this is considerably less headline-grabbing than animal sacrifice or ritual murder. And, of course, some people have been convicted of horrific acts nominally committed in the name of Satan. But these are hardly the first murders committed in a religion's name, and there is no evidence to suggest that such killers are more representative of Satanism than other religiously inspired murderers are of their faiths. And what of the Oklahoman Satanists' proposed statue? After a lengthy legal battle, the state Supreme Court ordered the removal of the Ten Commandants statue, on the basis that it violated the state's constitutional ban against the use of public property to benefit a religion. That meant the Satanists' monument would not be allowed either. They unveiled it in Detroit in July 2015, and have since been lobbying to have it installed in Arkansas. Like Oklahoma before it, it has voted to erect a Ten Commandments monument on the grounds of its state capitol, to the dismay of atheists, humanists – and Satanists, too.

Global curiosities: things some countries do differently

Why the French are so strict about Islamic head-coverings

The French breathed a collective sigh of relief on July 1st 2014 when the European Court of Human Rights upheld the country's 2010 ban on the wearing of full-faced veils in public places. It followed a separate ruling in June by a top French appeals court that a private day-care nursery was within its rights when it sacked an employee who refused to take off her Muslim headscarf at work. In France, such rules generate relatively little controversy. Yet they are often misunderstood in countries where liberal multiculturalism is the established creed. Why are the French so strict about Islamic head-coverings?

France adheres to a strict form of secularism, known as *laïcité*, which is designed to keep religion out of public life. This principle was entrenched by law in 1905, after fierce anti-clerical struggles with the Roman Catholic church. Today, the lines are in some ways blurred. The French maintain, for instance, certain Catholic public holidays, such as Ascension. But on the whole, secular rules prevail. It would be unthinkable in France, for example, to stage a nativity play in a state primary school, or for a president to be sworn in on a Bible.

Over the past 30 years, in response to a growing assertiveness among the country's 5 million–6 million Muslims, the focus of this effort to balance religious and secular needs has shifted to Islam. After a decade of legal uncertainty over the wearing of the headscarf in state schools, the French government in 2004 banned all "conspicuous" religious symbols, including the Muslim headscarf, from public institutions such as state schools or town halls. This was followed in 2010 by what the French call the "burqa ban", outlawing the full face covering in public. Critics accuse France of illiberalism, of curbing freedom of religious expression, and of imposing a Western interpretation of female oppression. Amnesty International, for example, called the 2014 European court ruling "a profound retreat for the right to freedom of expression and religion".

For the French, however, it is part of an unapologetic effort to keep religious expression private, and to uphold the country's republican secular identity. Interestingly, many moderate Muslim leaders also back the ban as a bulwark against hard-line Islam.

Had the European Court ruled against France, it would have prompted an outcry there. The country enjoys broad cross-party support for applying secular principles, on the left and the right, and the court accepted that it was part of France's effort to encourage a society based on "living together". If anything, the judgment will reinforce France's resolve to protect its secular tradition. The ruling against the day-care nursery employee was the first time that a ban on the Muslim headscarf was extended into the private sector. In its judgment, the court stressed that its ruling should not be generalised, as it related to the nursery's own company regulations. Yet a precedent was set, and the chances are that the French will in future enforce rather than loosen bans on Muslim head-coverings.

Why Japan leads the world in high-speed trains

Many countries seem obsessed with high-speed rail. Britain intends to build a controversial high-speed link known as HS2, connecting London to Birmingham, Manchester and Leeds. In California there are plans to build a high-speed link between San Francisco and Los Angeles. France is slowly expanding its high-speed lines (known as the TGV, for "trains de grande vitesse") while other countries, such as Spain and China, are enlarging their networks of whizzy trains more rapidly. Japan's high-speed "bullet" train is often held up as an exemplar by rail boosters and governments keen to acquire their own shiny new train-sets. How did Japan come to be the world leader in high-speed trains?

Trains symbolise modernity in Japan. During the Meiji restoration in the late 19th century, when Japan modernised at break-neck speed, the high technology of the day was the locomotive. By the 1930s the first railway trunk route, linking Tokyo with cities such as Nagoya, Kyoto, Osaka and Kobe, had become heavily congested. The first high-speed railway, known as the *Shinkansen* ("new mainline"), cut journeys between Tokyo and Osaka by two hours (from six to four) when it opened in 1964. This made it competitive with air travel, an industry which Japan had eschewed after the second world war, to avoid inadvertently stoking fears of rearmament.

Geography also influenced the rail network's development: most of Japan's 128 million inhabitants live in a few densely populated parts of the country. By linking those dense populations together – nearly 40 million people in greater Tokyo with 20 million residents of Osaka, Kobe and Kyoto – the railway helped to shift business patterns, making day trips between Tokyo and Osaka possible. Many of its customers were rich and willing to pay for more expensive high-speed tickets. The service had carried 100 million passengers within three years and 1 billion by 1976. Now around 143 million use the railway annually.

In 1987 Japan's national railways were divided and privatised into seven for-profit companies. JR East, the largest by passenger numbers, does not require any public subsidy from the Japanese government, unlike the heavily subsidised French network. One reason for its efficiency is that JR East owns all the infrastructure on the route – the stations, the rolling stock and the tracks – meaning there are fewer management teams duplicating each other's work. (By contrast in Britain, for instance, ownership of the tracks and trains is split up.) But the railway also thrives because of a planning system that encourages the building of commercial developments and housing alongside the railway route. JR East owns the land around the railways and lets it out; nearly a third of its revenue comes from shopping malls, blocks of offices, flats and the like. This money is reinvested in the network. In Britain, where planning and transport are rarely aligned, it is hard to create similarly successful commercial developments. Indeed, most of the plans for the areas around the stations of HS2 are vague, and some of the stops along an earlier line, HS1, are still underdeveloped, years after the line was built.

The ability to build large developments alongside the high-speed railways is a boon to the Japanese bullet line, as is the ability to charge high ticket prices. (When Koichi Tanaka, a scientist, won the Nobel Prize in 2002 he was reported as saying he would use the money to buy a ticket on the *Shinkansen*, to loud cheers.) But even so, 71% of the revenue from passenger tickets at JR East comes from the conventional, slower railway. High-speed trains are impressive. But countries looking to lay down speedy new tracks might want to consider investing in their existing railway lines as well.

More neighbours make more fences

Europe will soon have more physical barriers on its national borders than it did during the Cold War. The refugee crisis, and Ukraine's ongoing conflict with Russia, have prompted governments to plan and construct border walls and security fences across Mediterranean and eastern Europe. On September 15th 2015, Hungary completed a fence along its border with Serbia, a major point of entry for refugees making their way into the EU. Within hours, over 60 people were arrested for attempting to scale it. It was a further addition to a ring of anti-migrant fences built along the southern fringes of the EU's visa-free Schengen zone. In the mid-1990s, Spain fenced off its Moroccan enclaves of Ceuta and Melilla; in 2012 fences were erected on Greece's and Bulgaria's borders with Turkey. In northern Europe, platforms at Copenhagen's Kastrup rail station were fenced off in late 2015 as part of Sweden's latest effort to control the number of migrants entering Malmö from Denmark across the Oresund bridge. Ukraine began sealing off its border with Russia in 2014. In 2015, the Baltic states announced they were following suit. That would leave Belarus as the only country with an unsealed border between the Baltic and the Black sea.

Since the fall of the Berlin Wall, 40 countries around the world have built fences against 64 of their neighbours. Most have justified their actions on the basis of security concerns and the prevention of illegal migration. More than 30 of those decisions were made after 9/11. In the Middle East, the wars in Iraq, Afghanistan and Syria, and the associated wave of refugees, have prompted most countries to close borders. When it completes its border-wall with Jordan, Israel will have surrounded itself entirely. In Asia, too, walls and fences have proliferated, generally designed to prevent illicit movement of people and goods rather than to seal disputed borders, though Kashmir's line of control at India and Pakistan's disputed northern boundary remains a highly militarised example.

Some proposals for border fences are less plausible than others. In 2013 Brazil announced a "virtual" wall, monitored by drones and

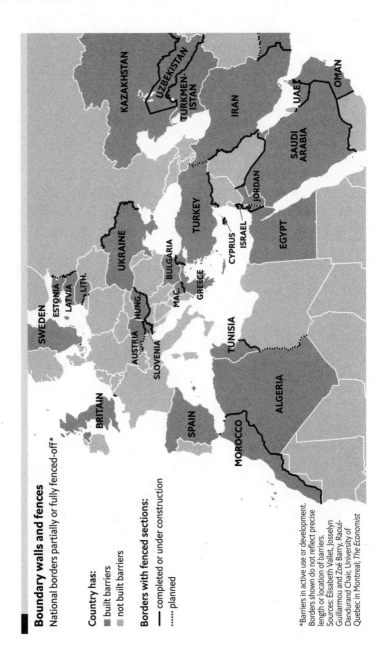

Boundary walls and fences
National borders partially or fully fenced-off*

Country has:

▓ built barriers

░ not built barriers

Borders with fenced sections:

— completed or under construction

⋯⋯ planned

*Barriers in active use or development.
Borders shown do not reflect precise
length or location of barriers.
Sources: Elisabeth Vallet, Josselyn
Guillarmou and Zoé Barry, Raoul-
Dandurand Chair, University of
Quebec in Montreal; The Economist

satellites, around its entire, nearly 15,000km (9,000 mile), border. It has begun work on the Paraguayan and Bolivian sections, which are hot-spots for smuggling. But sceptics point out that much of Brazil's border runs through rainforest that is impassable and hard to monitor. Even given easier terrain, high-tech border security often fails. Saudi Arabia, which has shuttered five of its borders since 2003, and the United States, which has several times fortified its border with Mexico, have struggled with proposals that were too expensive or didn't work – though nobody seems to have told Donald Trump. For most countries, barbed-wire or electric fences, combined with ditches and buffer zones, are the reality. Thankfully, unlike during the Cold War, transgressors of Europe's new borders are no longer shot.

Why North Korea turned back its clocks

It seemed appropriate for a nation that venerates its history and is stuck in the past: on August 15th 2015, everyone in North Korea went back in time, as they turned back their clocks by half an hour. The hermit kingdom already had its own calendar, with years counted from 1912, the birth year of its founder and "eternal president", Kim Il-sung. Changing the clocks means it now has its own time zone, too. Why did North Korea turn back its clocks?

Such time-travelling is the latest example of a long historical tradition of rulers expressing political power by adjusting clocks and calendars. Doing so alters a fundamental aspect of daily life, literally at a stroke. And what better illustration could there be of a ruler's might than control over time itself? Admittedly, not all such changes stand the test of time: French revolutionaries, keen to emphasise the break with their monarchist past, failed to get their ten-hour clock and entirely new calendar to stick after imposing them in 1793. The Soviet Union's experiments with five- and six-day weeks during the 1930s also failed to endure. But those changes that do persist can memorialise past rulers more effectively than any physical monument. July was named in honour of Julius Caesar in 45 BC, and August was later renamed after Augustus Caesar. They and their empire are long gone, but these two eminent Romans live on in the Western calendar.

In the modern era, control of time provides a way to underline the clout of central government: both India and China, despite their size, have a single time zone, which keeps everyone marching in step with the capital. It also offers an opportunity for emphasising independence and non-conformity. Hugo Chávez turned the clocks back by half an hour in 2007 to move Venezuela into its own time zone – supposedly to allow a "fairer distribution of the sunrise" but also ensuring that the socialist republic did not have to share a time zone with its arch-enemy, the United States. Perhaps the strangest example is that of Turkmenistan under President Saparmurat Niyazov, who renamed all the months and most of the days of the week in 2002, even renaming April after his mother. For its part, North Korea shifted its time zone to reverse the imposition of Tokyo time by "wicked Japanese imperialists" in 1912. South Korea did the same in 1954, but switched back to Japanese time in 1961 to encourage trade. North Korea's new time zone therefore extends the division of the Korean peninsula into the realm of time as well as space.

In theory, modern technology offers liberation from temporal tyranny, by allowing people to use the system they prefer. Smartphones and computers can seamlessly translate between time zones and calendar systems, allowing people to use whichever they like. In practice, however, time zones and calendars are more than just arbitrary ways to rule lines on time. They do not merely specify how to refer to a particular instant or period; they also dictate and co-ordinate activities across entire societies, in particular by defining which days are working days and national holidays. These have to be consistent within countries and, in some cases, between them: just ask Saudi Arabia, which in 2013 moved its weekend from Thursday/Friday to Friday/Saturday, to bring it into line with other Arab states. The need for such co-ordination means there is no escape from centralised control of clocks and calendars – which explains, in turn, why the tendency to tinker with them for political purposes is timeless.

Why so many American women die in childbirth

Childbirth was once a reliably dangerous experience. As late as the 1930s, one out of every 100 live births in the United States cost a woman her life; similar rates were seen around the world. But the 20th century brought tremendous advances in obstetric medicine and widened access to decent care. The maternal-mortality rate plummeted in rich countries by as much as 99%, and now poor countries are starting to catch up. But in America something odd is happening: over the past quarter of a century, the maternal-mortality rate (which counts deaths within 42 days after delivery) has been creeping back up. In 2013 more than 18 women died for every 100,000 live births. America is one of only eight countries, including Afghanistan and South Sudan, where these numbers are moving in the wrong direction. What is going on?

Some speculate that it has to do with the fact that American women tend to be both fatter and older when they become pregnant these days – and the risks associated with childbirth rise in tandem with weight and age. But similar trends can be seen in plenty of countries where the death rates are still coming down. Others suggest optimistically that America has become more rigorous about counting these deaths. The problem with this theory is that the system for collecting these records hasn't changed much over the past decade, yet the rate has continued to rise.

The most compelling explanation is that more women are in poorer health when they get pregnant, and then failing to get proper care. Chronic health problems, such as obesity, hypertension, diabetes and heart disease, are increasingly common among pregnant American women, and each of them makes delivery more dangerous. Indeed the traditional causes of pregnancy-related deaths, such as haemorrhage, venous thromboembolism and hypertensive disorders, have been declining in recent years, whereas deaths from cardiovascular conditions and other chronic problems have been on the rise. These conditions are more common among African-American women, which partly explains why they are nearly four times more likely to die from pregnancy-related complications than white women. Poverty is also closely correlated with worse health outcomes, as poor women are less likely to have access to proper health care, including contraception and prenatal care. (Women who become pregnant accidentally are also less likely to seek timely prenatal care, which raises the risks of death.) African-Americans are also more than twice as likely as their non-black peers to live below the poverty line, which helps to explain the grim racial disparity in maternal mortality rates.

What is the solution? Many hope the Affordable Care Act (ACA), otherwise known as Obamacare, will widen access to health care and ensure that more women are in better shape when they become pregnant. In the 31 states plus Washington, DC, that expanded Medicaid under the ACA, poorer women have access to contraception and better care before and after childbirth, which should reduce their mortality risks. (After-care is seen as essential for both managing potentially critical problems and putting women back on track for a healthy lifestyle.) Studies of obstetric emergencies have also shown that at least 40% of fatalities are completely avoidable in the moment. Once doctors are trained to spot the signs of haemorrhage, severe hypertension and venous thromboembolism when they arise, they can move more swiftly to protect their patients' lives. Federal, state and professional organisations, including the Centers for Disease Control and Prevention and the American College of Obstetricians and Gynecologists, are working together to make sure that hospitals and childbirth centres know how to handle these emergencies. Hospitals in California – where one in eight American births takes place – have put these protocols in place already, and the state has managed to bring its maternal-mortality rate down. The hope is to see a similar transformation on a national scale.

Which countries lose the most on gambling?

The gambling industry won a bit less money from the world's punters in 2014. Gross winnings (total take minus payouts, excluding expenses) are estimated to have dipped by 2.6% to $488 billion, according to H2 Gambling Capital, a British consultancy, partly because of China's corruption clampdown in Macau, where revenues have been tumbling. The industry's winnings are, of course, the punters' losses. Asia is home to the unluckiest punters on a per-adult basis. Australians gamble (and lose) the most: an estimated $1,130 for every adult in the country, due to a high propensity to gamble and an abundance of places to do so. A sizeable share of the losses are spent on "pokies" or video-poker machines. Australia has the highest concentration of such machines in the world, on which a person can lose over $1,500 an hour, though tighter regulation has seen the country fall to sixth place in absolute terms in recent years. A review of outdated regulations governing interactive gambling (sports betting and other games played on mobile phones, computers and so on) is under way. The law, enacted in 2001, is so ambiguous that some onshore operators have devised a novel way to skirt restrictions that specify that bets placed while a sporting event is happening must be made solely by telephone or in person and not online: they ask bettors to turn on their mobile-phone microphones, thus turning an online bet into a telephone one.

Elsewhere, big-spending gamblers in America and Singapore splash their cash in casinos. In tech-savvy and open markets such as Finland, Ireland and Norway, interactive betting is most popular. America remains the world's biggest market, but its global share is steadily being eroded, partly because of a ban on most interactive gambling. Despite the crackdown in Macau, which began in 2014, China is still a growing market, climbing from the tenth- to the second-largest in a decade, with national losses including its territories of Macau and Hong Kong amounting to $95 billion.

Taking a punt
2014 estimate

Biggest gamblers, loss per resident adult, $

■ Gaming machines *(non-casino)*   ■ Casino & betting   ■ Lotteries, interactive* & other

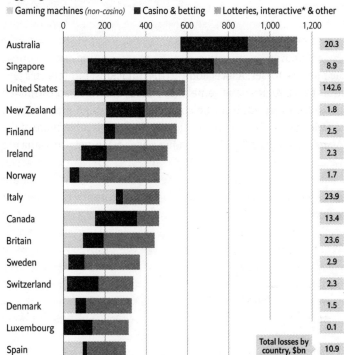

Australia	20.3
Singapore	8.9
United States	142.6
New Zealand	1.8
Finland	2.5
Ireland	2.3
Norway	1.7
Italy	23.9
Canada	13.4
Britain	23.6
Sweden	2.9
Switzerland	2.3
Denmark	1.5
Luxembourg	0.1
Spain	10.9

Total losses by country, $bn

Biggest losses by country, $bn

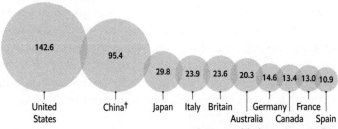

United States	China†	Japan	Italy	Britain	Australia	Germany	Canada	France	Spain
142.6	95.4	29.8	23.9	23.6	20.3	14.6	13.4	13.0	10.9

Sources: H2 Gambling Capital; Thomson Reuters

*Computer, mobile phone or interactive TV
†Includes Special Administrative Regions

What China means by "democracy"

In 2014, Tony Abbott, then the prime minister of Australia, embarrassed himself a little by gushing over Chinese President Xi Jinping's talk of China becoming "democratic". Specifically Mr Xi said China had the goal of becoming "a modern socialist country that is prosperous, democratic, culturally advanced and harmonious" by the middle of the 21st century. Mr Abbott responded in wonderment that he had never before heard of a Chinese leader promising full democracy by 2050. He could have done with an explanation of what China's leader means by "democracy". What did Mr Xi really mean?

Chinese official language is full of political terms that, to the Western liberal ear, sound progressive. The Chinese government has long said it protects "human rights". It has a Western-sounding constitution that says the country enjoys the "freedom of speech, of the press, of assembly" and so on. In October 2014, the Communist Party's Central Committee held a plenary session on "rule of law", in which it fully endorsed the constitution. But China prefers a narrow economic definition of "human rights", and none of these declared freedoms, nor the authority of the constitution itself, goes so far as to protect anyone who challenges the Communist Party's rule. Ilham Tohti, a university professor, was sentenced to life imprisonment in 2014 for criticising the party's ethnic policies.

The word "democracy", or "minzhu", is relatively new in Chinese, added to the language by Japanese writers during Japan's Meiji Restoration more than a century ago (along with the word "freedom", or "ziyou"). In the early 1900s "democracy" had the same meaning as it did in the West – and after the fall of the Qing dynasty China even held real elections in 1912–13. But democracy didn't stick. The victor of those polls, Song Jiaoren, was assassinated before he could become prime minister, and decades of turmoil and civil war followed. In leading the communists to power Mao incorporated the word "democracy" into party-speak to gain popular support. But what Mao actually meant in 1949 became clear when he declared that China would be ruled by a "people's democratic dictatorship".

Incorporated into the first line of the constitution, that phrase is still very much in use today. It also says that the country's legislators are chosen through "democratic elections" and that its state-owned enterprises "practise democratic management through congresses of workers and staff". This is socialist democracy in the sense that the party believes itself to represent the people. None of this bears any resemblance to Western democracy and its institutions. Mr Xi has made clear that Western-style democracy is not for China, and under his leadership authorities have cracked down hard on lawyers and intellectuals who have pushed for constitutional and democratic rights. Independent political parties are banned. That said, there is a chance that the "democratic" China of the future may look different from how it looks now. The Communist Party tinkers from time to time with democratic concepts around the edges, experiments that in theory could lead to, say, a Singapore-style government where popular elections are held, but one party dominates. By 2050, perhaps real democracy could even be flourishing in China with the blessing of a future Communist Party leader. But for now the "democratic" China Mr Xi has in mind is very different from how Westerners understand the word.

Why some Indian castes are demanding lower status

In late February 2016, the citizens of Delhi were made painfully aware of a grievance borne by the Jats of Haryana, a state that surrounds India's capital on three sides. The Jats are a caste-like community spread from Pakistan across much of north India. They are particularly strong in Haryana, where they make up a quarter of the population. Yet Haryana's Jats are angry. They are jealous that weaker, lower-caste groups get government aid, and they want to be classified as equally deserving. Protests that started peacefully soon turned violent as rioters looted, pillaged and raped, and blocked roads, railways and a canal that supplies about half of Delhi's water. Other castes in other parts of India have staged similar protests over the past year, several of which have turned violent. Why do they want so badly to be reclassified?

Since India's independence, the government has made provisions to uplift the most downtrodden members of the caste system, known as Dalits, most often by means of state favours known as "reservations": jobs and slots at universities set aside for the people who had been least likely to enjoy their benefits. None of the riots has been started by Dalits, who were traditionally known as "untouchables". It is relatively clear who counts as a Dalit: about a quarter of the country's population qualifies, including remote tribal groups. But since 1990 the national government has allowed other, somewhat less disadvantaged groups to claim similar benefits, if they can establish that they belong to the so-called "Other Backward Classes" (OBCs). There are 11 formal criteria for admission into the ranks of the OBCs, but these are open to interpretation. Dalits and OBCs together may claim as many as 50% of a given state's reservations. The Jats of Haryana, like the Patidars of Gujarat or the Kapus of Andhra Pradesh, all want to be counted among the OBCs to gain a slice of the social-welfare pie to which lowlier castes are entitled.

The perverse thing about the current crop of OBC-seekers is that each is already what sociologists define as a "dominant caste". In their native states they own much of the land and have the political and economic power that comes with it. Marathas have even given their name to a state – Maharashtra – in which they now want to be regarded as an OBC. In some cases their leaders are aware that their own groups are not among the most deserving of government support. But they don't want to miss out on the benefits that accrue from being deemed to be in the bottom half, and they have the numbers to get their way. Speaking candidly, leaders of the Patidar movement admitted they would rather see the whole system of reservations scrapped. But, thinking that unfeasible, they say they'll pursue the more modest goal of gathering some fraction of the goodies to their own kind.

This twisted logic now looks like an inevitable consequence of the decisions made in 1990. But the immediate problem facing people like Haryana's Jats, who are farmers by custom, is an economic crisis. Their state is one of India's more prosperous. But farming is no longer a good way to earn a decent income, and most of their sons lack the education that could make them employable in an increasingly urban society. In some areas this has inspired desperate hopes for the security of a government job, or a technical education, via membership in a caste. When they rioted, Haryana's Jats attacked Sainis, a recognised OBC – but they also besieged a string of factories that connect their state to Delhi, halting production at a Maruti-Suzuki car plant. They want education and jobs. The quirks of India's caste system just give them an unusual way to make their demands.

How Asians view each other

Old resentments die hard in Asia. A report by the Pew Research Centre on public perceptions in countries in the Asia-Pacific region bears this out. Historic grudges continue to colour the views East Asians in particular (in China, Japan and South Korea) hold about the other countries. Seventy years after Japan's second-world-war surrender and the end of its occupation of much of China, very few Chinese see Japan in a favourable light. Correspondingly, as China has been increasingly assertive in pursuing its territorial dispute with Japan over the Senkaku or Diaoyu islands, the number of Japanese with positive views of China has fallen to similar levels.

The end of the second world war also marked the end of Japanese colonial rule in Korea. Many South Koreans, like many Chinese, still believe that Japan has not apologised enough for its militaristic, colonial past. Today just 25% of South Koreans view Japan favourably. Elsewhere, however, although many other parts of Asia suffered Japanese aggression, much of the region has a generally positive image of Japan. In Malaysia, for example, also occupied by Japan during the war, 84% of those surveyed view Japan kindly. So too in South Asia, where both Indians and Pakistanis hold favourable views of Japan (and reserve their deepest resentments for each other).

China, meanwhile, remains very popular with its "all-weather friend" Pakistan. And overall, a majority of those surveyed (57%) held favourable views of the biggest power in the region. But some countries, particularly those bordering the South China Sea, felt much more wary. They are alarmed by China's frenzied construction activity in the sea, turning rocks and reefs into artificial islands that could have military uses. When asked about China's overlapping territorial claims, the vast majority of people in the Philippines and Vietnam – where the disputes are most active – said they were "very or somewhat concerned". A majority of Indians, Japanese and South Koreans – all with their own territorial disagreements with China – are also worried.

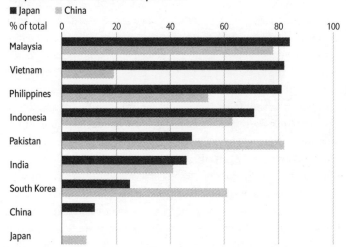

Asian opinion
April–May 2015

Respondents with a favourable opinion of:

■ Japan ▨ China

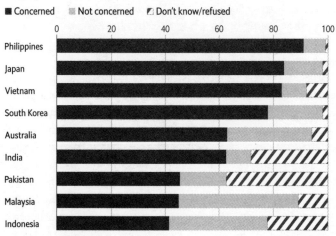

Views of territorial disputes with China
% saying

■ Concerned ▨ Not concerned ▨ Don't know/refused

Source: Pew Research Centre

Why Saudi Arabians love social media so much

By most counts the Gulf region has the highest penetration of smartphones in the world. WhatsApp, Facebook and Twitter have become standard modes of communication. Nowhere is this more so than in Saudi Arabia. Several surveys in 2013 showed that the kingdom has the world's highest percentage of people on Twitter relative to its number of internet users; and on YouTube, too. Saudis also spend more hours online than their peers elsewhere. That might seem surprising for such a conservative country where the constitution is said to be taken directly from the Koran and where women are not permitted to drive. Why are Saudis such big fans of social media?

Outsiders often regard the 30 million Saudis as far behind the rest of the world. The modern Saudi state was founded only in 1932, and then on the basis of an existing pact between the Al Saud family and the Wahhabist clerics, who peddle a particularly red-hot version of Islam. It is certainly a traditional place, especially around the capital Riyadh. But the country has also rapidly modernised since discovering its vast oil wealth. It has a GDP per capita of almost $26,000. Today thousands of its young people study abroad, speak English and are as globalised as their peers in other countries. Fully 75% of the population are under 30. They have grown up thinking it normal to go online to do everything from ordering a coffee to watching TV.

It is the wedding of these factors to Saudi Arabia's social peculiarities that may account for its topping of the virtual rankings. Shopping malls are pretty much the only source of entertainment for young people, because the clerics dislike cinemas and bars. So mingling with friends on social media has obvious appeal, not least because it is illegal for unrelated men and women to fraternise in person. Facebook has become a way of picking up a date (previously, many young people would turn on Bluetooth and search for random connections nearby). Frustrated Saudis can also vent about the government anonymously on Twitter. But social media is not just used for getting up to naughty things. The country's most popular Twitter account, with more than 14 million followers, is that of Muhammad al-Arefe, a Saudi cleric – and not a particularly liberal one, either.

Saudi rulers make occasional attempts to close down social media or to criminalise things said in cyberspace – often with harsh punishments. Clerics, including salafist-jihadists, use the internet and social-media apps to spread their message to the vast swathe of the population that is devout and, as such, potentially susceptible to their ideas. But it is impossible to stem enthusiasm for all things online. On the whole, most observers reckon social media is more of a force for liberalisation. And there is no sign that the appetite for it is slowing. Saudis are becoming creators as well as consumers of social media content and services. Saudi entrepreneurs, especially in the more relaxed Red Sea city of Jeddah, are launching apps and YouTube channels. Whatever the position of Saudis in the real world, they are fully integrated in the virtual one.

How Europeans view each other

What do Europeans think about each other? When the Pew Research Centre asked people in eight European countries about their attitudes to one another in 2013, the results were revealing, exposing lingering stereotyping, some historical mistrust and a bit of modern-day resentment about economic power. The survey also appeared to confirm a puzzling finding from a similar Pew survey carried out in 2012: that Greeks' perception of themselves is out of kilter with everyone else's.

As the table shows, when asked to name the most trustworthy nation, every country voted for Germany except for the Greeks. Instead, they awarded themselves that accolade, while casting Germany as the most arrogant and least compassionate nation. (In the 2012 poll, Greeks considered themselves to be the most hardworking, to general bemusement.) This antipathy towards Germany is understandable. As the main paymaster for the euro area, Germany is blamed for the strict austerity measures imposed on Greece as a condition for bailing out the country. These have resulted in a cycle of declining growth, weakening demand and real hardship. Indeed, Germany's economic dominance is reflected in its

Who is trustworthy, arrogant or compassionate?
EU nation most frequently cited as top choice by other country

Viewed by:	TRUSTWORTHY		ARROGANT		COMPASSIONATE	
	most	least	most	least	most	least
Britain	Germany	France	France	Britain	Britain	Germany
France	Germany	Greece	France	France	France	Britain
Germany	Germany	Greece/Italy	France	Germany	Germany	Britain
Italy	Germany	Italy	Germany	Spain	Italy	Germany
Spain	Germany	Italy	Germany	Spain	Spain	Germany
Greece	Greece	Germany	Germany	Greece	Greece	Germany
Poland	Germany	Germany	Germany	Poland	Poland	Germany
Czech Rep.	Germany	Greece	Germany	Slovakia	Czech Rep.	Germany

Source: Pew Research Centre

several nominations as the most arrogant and least compassionate country.

Another striking finding is the dichotomy of opinion within countries. The Poles nominated Germany as both the most and least trustworthy nation, possibly dividing among older Poles with memories of war and younger ones who admire its reputation for prudence. The French, too, appear to be in two minds about their own arrogance – though the Brits are in no doubt about it. In a telling answer, Italians are most mistrustful of one another, perhaps aware that their country ranks badly on international corruption measures. Slovaks may not know whether to be (quietly) proud or slightly miffed that they are named the most humble nation by their neighbours and one-time compatriots, the Czechs.

Where the Maltese language comes from

It may seem surprising that a dialect of Arabic is an official language of the European Union. But travel 90km south of Sicily and the odd-sounding language of the EU's smallest state, Malta, is exactly that. With some 450,000 native speakers, Maltese was granted official status in 2004 after the country joined the EU. Malta also belongs to the Commonwealth. Its language is the sole survivor of the Arabic dialects spoken in Spain and Sicily in the Middle Ages and the only Semitic language written in the Latin script. When spoken, Maltese sounds like Arabic with a sprinkling of English phrases. When written it looks like Italian with a blend of some peculiar symbols. So where does modern Maltese come from?

Much like its society, Malta's language is the result of centuries of cultural mingling. From as early as the ninth century until 1964, when the country became independent, a series of conquerors left their mark on all aspects of Maltese life, from architecture and the arts to the island's colourful cuisine. The main linguistic transformation came in around 1050, when the ruling Arabs absorbed the existing community and, through force of numbers, replaced the local tongue with their own. The Sicilians and the Knights of Malta followed. Sicilian, Latin and Italian, which was later declared the country's official language, enjoyed high status for centuries – but Arabic persisted. In 1800 Malta became a British colony, and English, which joined the existing Babel of languages, gradually prevailed over its linguistic rivals.

Maltese developed in parallel with the nationalities of those who ruled it, absorbing new elements and fitting them into its simplified Arabic structures. Even after the British named it a national language in 1934, it was affected by foreign elements. Along with Maltese, English remained (and still is) one of the country's two official languages; and until 1959 television was only available in Italian. The resulting polyglot culture is at the heart of Malta's modern society. According to a Eurobarometer poll in 2012, some 90% of the island's population speak English. Another

36% speak Italian. Half of the subjects in the country's schools and almost all of its university courses are taught in English. Shop signs and menus are in English and Italian; newspapers in English and Maltese.

Identity and language are closely entwined, but the high level of bilingualism in Malta has made code-switching rife. The use of English is increasingly present in informal speech – some words are even adopted and given a new life in Italian forms. Some fear this intrusion could cause the language to be abandoned. Others dismiss such concerns as irrelevant. Professor Joseph Brincat, who teaches linguistics at the University of Malta, says it is too early to say whether Maltese will survive. But whereas Malta's tongue emerged through inescapable blending, it is no longer vulnerable to the whims of foreign rulers. Like its booming economy, the evolution of the island's language depends on those who speak it.

Why the Japanese are having fewer babies

In 2014, a local official in Aichi prefecture set out a daring proposal. Tomonaga Osada suggested that the authorities could distribute secretly punctured condoms to young married couples, who would then get to work boosting the birth rate. His unorthodox ploy won few supporters, yet it reflected growing concern about Japan's demographic plight. In 2014, just over 1 million babies were born, far fewer than the number needed to maintain the population, which is expected to drop from 127 million to around 87 million by 2060. Why are young Japanese so loth to procreate?

The spiral of demographic decline is spinning faster as the number of women of child-bearing age falls. Some 500 towns across the country are expected to disappear by 2040 as young women migrate to bigger cities. The workforce is already shrinking, endangering future growth. In recent years governments have embarked on a plethora of schemes to encourage childbearing, including a "women's handbook" to educate young females on the high and low points of their fertility, and state-sponsored matchmaking events.

The chief reason for the dearth of births is the decline of marriage. Fewer people are opting to wed, and those who do are getting married later in life. At least a third of young women aim to become full-time housewives, yet they struggle to find men who can support a traditional family. In better economic times potential suitors had permanent jobs as part of Japan's "lifetime employment" system. Now many of them have to rely on temporary or part-time work. Other women shun marriage and children because Japan's old-fashioned corporate culture, together with a dire shortage of child care, forces them to give up their careers if they have children. Finally, young people are bound by strict social codes. Only around 2% of babies are born outside marriage (compared with 30–50% in most of the rich world), which means that as weddings plummet, so do births. And even for those who do start families, the rising cost of child-rearing often imposes a de facto one-child policy.

There is little the government can do directly to boost

productivity in the bedroom. Yet labour-market reforms could make a difference to the birth rate in the long term. If companies gave more protection to new, young hires and reduced the privileges of other employees, young couples would have a more stable basis on which to marry and raise families. The government of Shinzo Abe has talked about such steps, but has shied away from taking them. Instead Mr Abe is acting to help women combine careers with child-rearing. Many demographers reckon it is already too late to lift Japan's birth rate, now at 1.41 children per woman. The eventual answer, they say, will be even more shocking to Japanese society than sabotaged prophylactics: mass immigration.

The world's most innovative countries

Which is the world's most innovative country? Answering this question is the aim of the annual Global Innovation Index and a related report published by Cornell University, the international business school INSEAD and the World Intellectual Property Organisation. The ranking of 140 countries and economies around the world, which are scored using 79 indicators, is not surprising: Switzerland, Britain, Sweden, the Netherlands and the US lead the pack. But the authors also look at their data from other angles, for instance how countries do relative to their economic development and the quality of innovation (measured by indicators such as university rankings, patents filed per unit of GDP, and cited articles as a proportion of published articles). The report found that middle-income countries, led by China, still lag behind rich countries when it comes to innovation quality, but are narrowing the gap, thanks mainly to an improvement in the quality of their higher-education institutions. Although India has steadily improved its quality of innovation score, China has done so more rapidly: it is pulling ahead of the other middle-income countries and closing the gap with high-income countries. It is notable that middle-income countries depend heavily on the ranking of their universities to achieve their high rankings for quality of innovation. If they are to continue making progress in promoting innovation, they will have to pay more attention to the calibre of their academic publications, and boost the number of patents filed globally – the area where they are weakest.

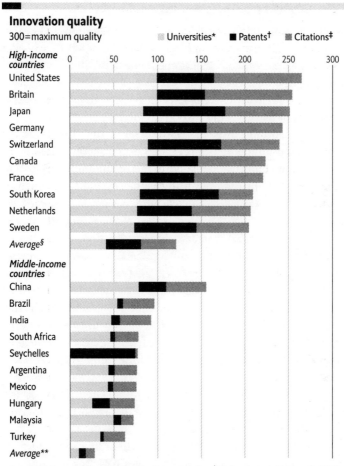

Innovation quality

300=maximum quality   Universities* ■ Patents† Citations‡

Source: Global   *Average rating of top three universities †Number of patents filed per unit of GDP
Innovation Index, 2015   ‡Cited articles as % of published articles §Of 48 countries **Of 72 countries

Why pigs are so important to China

Of all the meat options, pork reigns supreme in China. To keep up with demand, the country now rears (and eats) nearly 500 million pigs a year – more than half of all the swine in the whole world. But the significance of pork goes deeper than culinary tastes. Pigs have been at the centre of Chinese culture, cuisine and family life for thousands of years. So why are pigs so important to China?

Historically, sacrificial pigs featured in all forms of commemoration, including weddings, funerals and festivals. In Mandarin, the character for "family" is a pig under a roof. But up until recently, pork was pricey and scarce. Most people ate it only a few times a year. As China became richer over the past three decades, however, meat became a symbol of wealth. Consumption of meat, and pork in particular, soared: it comprises 70% of all meat eaten in China today. Since the government liberalised agriculture in the late 1970s, swine consumption has increased more than sevenfold.

The government has backed China's cultural love of pork with determined efforts to intensify pig production and keep plates piled high with cheap meat. The Chinese Communist Party regards keeping pork affordable and plentiful as an important way of maintaining societal stability. Because the Chinese eat so much pork, when the price of it rises, all prices rise. So the government supports pig farmers with huge subsidies. China also has the world's only strategic pork reserve – both live and frozen – to try to keep prices stable.

In addition, demand for pork is driving Chinese investment abroad. By one count, Chinese companies have bought 5 million hectares of land, more than half the size of Portugal, for food production, including pig farming, in other countries. In 2013, China's largest pork producer bought Smithfield Foods, the world's largest hog farmer and pork processor. It was the biggest Chinese takeover of an American company at the time. Chinese pigs are only going to have a greater impact in the future. China's per-capita meat consumption is still far lower than carnivorous nations such as Australia or America.

Why are so many adults adopted in Japan?

America and Japan top the charts for the highest rates of adoption – but with one big difference. Whereas the vast majority of adoptees in America are youngsters, in Japan children represent a tiny 2% of all adoptions. Men in their 20s and 30s make up the remaining 98%, or almost 90,000 adoptees in 2008 (up from fewer than 80,000 in 2000). Why are so many adults adopted in Japan?

The reason is more mercantile than magnanimous. Business acumen and skill are not reliably hereditary. As a result, most family businesses wilt after their founder's death. Just 37 members make up Les Hénokiens, a fraternity of companies worldwide that are at least 200 years old and are still run by a family member. The two firms which vie for the title of the world's oldest family company are Hoshi, an inn founded in 781, and Kongo Gumi, a Buddhist temple builder from 578 – and both are Japanese.

Before the second world war, Japan's civil code decreed that family wealth passed along male lines; tradition dictated it went to the eldest son. In daughter-only households, this fuelled a demand for adopted sons who could carry on the family name and business. (If a biological son was deemed an unsuitable heir, he too could be bypassed for an adopted one.) In turn, families with a surplus of younger sons sent them out for adoption. Many legal adoptions are coupled with a form of arranged marriage (known as *omiai*) to one of the family's daughters – but the son-in-law (or *mukoyoshi*) then changes his name to hers. Today a host of matchmaking companies and marriage consultants recruit voluntary adoptees for Japanese companies.

Although Japan's post-war code no longer upholds primogeniture, business families find the habit hard to kick. The country's declining birth rate has further limited the likelihood of a male heir for many of them; bosses often select sons from among their most promising top managers. The family owners of Toyota and Suzuki, both carmakers, Canon, an electronics firm, and Kajima, a construction company, have all adopted sons to manage them. Incentives are high for prospective adoptees, too. Their birth parents sometimes receive gifts of many million yen. To be selected as a *mukoyoshi* is to be awarded a high executive honour. This prompts fierce competition among managers, ensuring that the business has access to as good a talent pool as non-family companies. In fact, researchers have found that adopted heirs' firms outperform blood heirs' firms – although the prospect of being overlooked for an outsider can serve as motivation for sons to knuckle down, too.

By the numbers: economical with the truth

Health-care spending: America's longevity gap

The United States remains the world's most profligate spender on health care, according to a report published in November 2015 by the OECD, a club of 34 mostly rich countries. In 2013 the US spent, on average, $8,713 per person on health care – two and a half times as much as the OECD average. Yet the average American dies 1.7 years earlier than the average OECD citizen. This longevity gap has grown by a year since 2003. Americans have the same life expectancy as Chileans, even though Chile spends less than a fifth of what the US spends on health care per person. If health-care spending is supposed to increase life expectancy, then the US is not getting value for money.

Right nation

Health spending and life expectancy at birth
OECD countries

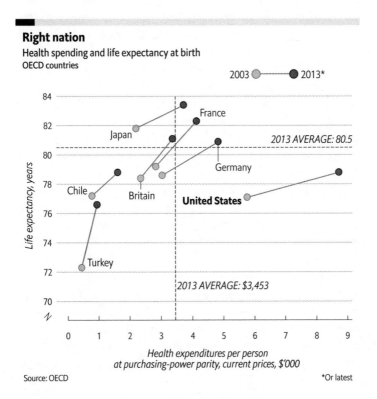

Source: OECD

*Or latest

Why lesbians earn more than straight women

Everyone knows that labour markets are not fair. Whether it is skin colour, gender or some other characteristic, minority groups tend to fare worse than the one group that, at least on average, seems to live life on the "easy" setting – white, well-educated men. For every dollar earned by a white, non-Hispanic man in full-time work, the average white woman in America earns 78 cents, and an average Hispanic woman only 56 cents. Gay men are no exception to this: even taking into account the influence of factors like education and experience, they earn less on average than straight men: around 5% less in France and Britain, and 12–16% in Canada and America. But one minority group seems to do better than others: lesbians. Why?

Research into this area is tricky; getting decent data is hard, and asking people to reveal their sexual orientation can be even harder. But studies across the world (in Canada, the US, Germany, Britain and the Netherlands) tend to uncover the same phenomenon; while gay men suffer an earnings penalty, gay women seem to earn more than straight women. In a survey of 29 studies published in January 2015, Marieka Klawitter of the University of Washington found an average earnings premium of 9% for lesbians over heterosexual women, compared with a penalty of 11% for gay men.

Establishing with certainty why this premium exists may be an impossible task, but various theories have emerged. One possibility is that lesbians might face positive discrimination, perhaps if employers expect them to be more competitive and more committed to work than their straight female colleagues. One study did find that in the (less heavily regulated) private sector, the penalty for gay men was heavier and the premium for lesbians was larger, which is consistent with this theory. Another idea is that lesbians are responding to the gender of their likely partner. They might have to work harder to plump up household income in the absence of a male partner. Or, it could be that in same-sex couples women find it easier to shrug off expectations that they will take on the bulk of child care or household chores. Same-sex couples do seem more likely to be dual-earners, even when there are children, and they also appear to share chores more equally than different-sex ones.

If this last theory is the correct one, then it could be that lesbians do in fact face discrimination in the labour market – just not as much as heterosexual women, so it shows up as a wage premium. But lesbians are not a privileged group. Qualitative studies have found that they face discrimination in hiring processes relative to heterosexual women. And although they might earn more than straight women, they still earn less than men. Poverty rates among lesbian couples are 7.9%, compared with 6.6% among different-sex couples. For boosting earnings, as in so many realms, nothing beats being a straight, white, married man.

What will the world's population look like in 2050?

Population forecasts from the United Nations point to a new world order in 2050. The number of people will grow from 7.3 billion to 9.7 billion in 2050, 100 million more than was estimated in the UN's previous report, released in 2013. More than half of this growth will come from Africa, where the population is set to double to 2.5 billion. Nigeria's population will reach 413 million, overtaking the US to become the world's third-most-populous country. Congo and Ethiopia will swell to more than 195 million and 188 million respectively, more than twice their current numbers.

India will surpass China as the world's most populous country in 2022, six years earlier than previously forecast. China's population will peak at 1.4 billion in 2028; India's four decades later at 1.75 billion. Changes in fertility make long-term projections hard, but by 2100 the planet's population will be rising past 11.2 billion. It will also be much older. The median age of 30 will rise to 36 in 2050 and 42 in 2100 – the median age of Europeans today. A quarter of Europe's people are already aged 60 or more; by 2050 deaths will outnumber births by 32 million. The UN warns that only migration will prevent the region's population from shrinking further.

In other parts of the world, conversely, young populations present an opportunity for countries to capture a demographic dividend, as the number of people in the working-age population surges, driving economic growth. In Africa, 41% of the population are under 15, and 60% are under 24. In Latin America and Asia, which have seen greater declines in fertility, the fractions of the population under 24 are 43% and 40% respectively. This presents an economic opportunity, provided policymakers can meet the challenges of delivering sufficient health care, education and jobs.

The world's population

Regional % change, 2015–50 forecast

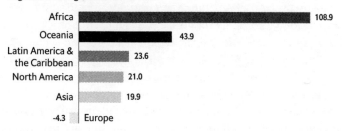

Africa	108.9
Oceania	43.9
Latin America & the Caribbean	23.6
North America	21.0
Asia	19.9
-4.3 Europe	

Total population, bn

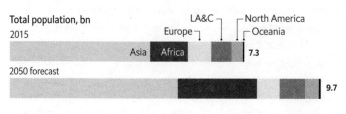

2015 — Europe, Asia, Africa, LA&C, North America, Oceania — 7.3

2050 forecast — 9.7

Most populous countries, bn

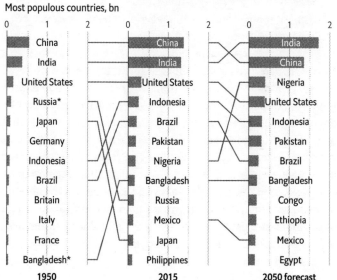

1950	2015	2050 forecast
China	China	India
India	India	China
United States	United States	Nigeria
Russia*	Indonesia	United States
Japan	Brazil	Indonesia
Germany	Pakistan	Pakistan
Indonesia	Nigeria	Brazil
Brazil	Bangladesh	Bangladesh
Britain	Russia	Congo
Italy	Mexico	Ethiopia
France	Japan	Mexico
Bangladesh*	Philippines	Egypt

Sources: UN; *The Economist*

*Did not exist as countries in 1950.
Historical estimates made using modern borders

Why big banknotes may be on the way out

High-value banknotes have been getting a lot of bad press. In February 2016 the European Central Bank announced an investigation into the use of the €500 ($549) note; soon afterwards Peter Sands of Harvard University published a report arguing for its withdrawal, along with big bills like the SFr1,000 note ($1,000) and even the $100 bill. Why are big banknotes falling out of favour?

For most people, large notes can be a liability, rather than an asset. Swanky shops in central Zurich will accept large notes in payment for posh fountain pens, though they use special machines to check they are not fakes. But try to pay for a taxi ride or a chocolate bar with a large note and you will be met by funny looks at best, and a flat-out refusal at worst. Most places will not accept them, and most Europeans have not even set eyes on a €500 note. Despite this, central bank statistics reveal that they are peculiarly popular: 60% of Swiss francs in circulation are in the form of SFr1,000 notes, and 30% of cash euros are in €500 notes. Some suspect that most high-denomination notes are in the hands not of anxious savers, but of criminals.

Working out exactly who holds cash is a tricky business; that, after all, is part of its attraction to lawbreakers. But law enforcers are sure that large notes are criminals' currency of choice, being compact and easy to hide. Recently, concerns have arisen over the role of large bills in financing terrorism: a courier for jihadists caught travelling to Turkey in 2014 with 40 €500 bills (€20,000) in her underwear would have needed very much larger knickers to transport the same sum using €100 notes. But David Lewis of the Financial Action Task Force, an international body that co-ordinates efforts to prevent criminals using the financial system, says high-value notes are used mainly in drug- and people-trafficking, money-laundering and racketeering. Mr Sands also argues that withdrawing them could help fill government coffers, by making tax-evading cash-in-hand payments harder.

Getting rid of large notes might also hinder criminals: bulky piles of cash are easier to spot. But the process is not straightforward.

Any withdrawal would have to be slow: central banks worry that putting an expiry date on cash could undermine the value of their currency. This will disappoint those hoping that eliminating high-value notes will prompt awkward conversations between criminals and the authorities. There is political resistance too; some worry that abolishing large notes might be a step on the road to abolishing paper money altogether. And without a coordinated withdrawal of all such notes, the move would be much less effective. The Swiss authorities have no plans to get rid of their Sfr1,000 note. But big-bill haters argue that in the business of making life harder for criminals, every little helps.

Why prostitutes are lowering their prices

The Economist analysed 190,000 profiles of female sex workers on websites where customers post reviews. The data cover 84 cities in 12 countries, with the biggest number of workers in America and most of the rest in big cities in rich countries. According to the analysis, the price of an hour of sex with a female prostitute has been dropping fairly steadily in recent years. In 2006 the average cost was around $340. By 2014 it had dropped to about $260.

A prostitute's hourly rate depends on a variety of factors, including the services she provides and her reported physical characteristics. Those who conform most closely to the stereotypical version of Western beauty – slim, with long blonde hair and full breasts – earn the most. Those who provide niche services – for example, sex workers who will accept two male clients at once – also command a premium. Location matters too. Prostitutes in San Francisco, where the cost of living is high, charge more than those in cheaper cities such as Prague.

The fall in prices can be attributed in part to the 2007–08 financial crisis. Even places that have escaped its worst effects, such as London, have been hit. In cities such as Cleveland, Ohio, where unemployment peaked at 12.5% in 2010, prices have plummeted. Migration is also driving down prices. Big, rich cities, such as London, attract a steady inward flow of poorer migrants, who are prepared to do all kinds of work for lower wages than locals. In places such as Norway, where local prostitutes had tried to standardise prices, growing numbers of migrant sex workers have made such unofficial price controls harder to sustain. The increase in people selling sex online – where it is easier to be anonymous – has probably boosted local supply. Meanwhile broader social changes may have reduced demand. Casual and adulterous sex is easier to find than in the past. Pre-marital sex is more acceptable and divorce easier, with the result that fewer frustrated single and married men turn to prostitutes. That drives prices down, too.

Sex workers complain that they are earning less than in the

past. But their incomes may not have fallen as steeply as the decline in prices would suggest. The shift towards advertising and coordinating the sale of sex online means that prostitutes now rely less on intermediaries, such as brothels and agencies, pimps and madams. As a result, they may be able to keep a greater proportion of their income. But selling sex online brings new demands. Clients contact sex workers via their websites, by e-mail, through Facebook and Twitter. Some websites allow prostitutes to tell clients whether they are currently available; but that means going online frequently to update their status. Such work is time-consuming, so some prostitutes may end up paying someone to do it for them. For sex workers, as much as anyone, time really is money.

The economics of Panini football stickers

Panini, an Italian firm, has produced sticker albums for World Cups since the tournament in Mexico in 1970; in 2014, there were 640 stickers to collect. The market for the stickers is not just for kids, however; it is also for micro-economists. Getting every slot filled delivers an early lesson in probability; the value of statistical tests; the laws of supply and demand; and the importance of liquidity.

When you start an album, your first sticker (they come in packs of five) has a 640/640 probability of being one you don't have already. As the spaces get filled, however, the odds of opening a pack and finding a sticker you want lengthen. According to Sylvain Sardy and Yvan Velenik, two mathematicians at the University of Geneva, the number of sticker packs that you would have to buy on average to fill the album by mechanically buying pack after pack would be 899. That assumes there is no supply shock to the market: the theft of 300,000 stickers in Brazil in April 2014 left many collectors fearful that Panini would run short of cards.

It also assumes that the market is not being rigged. Panini insists that each sticker is printed in the same volume and randomly distributed. But many collectors will be haunted by a single recurrent card. In a 2010 analysis, Messrs Sardy and Velenik played the role of "regulator" by checking the distribution of stickers for a 660-sticker album sold in Switzerland for that year's World Cup. Out of their sample of 6,000 stickers, they expected to see each sticker 9.09 times on average (6,000/660). They tested to see whether the actual fluctuations around this number were consistent with the expected distribution of stickers, and found that it was. Such statistical tests are increasingly being applied to spot price-fixing and anti-competitive behaviour in financial markets, too.

Even in a fair market, though, it is inefficient to buy pack after pack as an individual (not to mention hugely expensive for parents). The answer is to create a market for collectors to swap their unwanted stickers. The playground is one version of this market, where a child who has a card prized by many suddenly understands the power of limited supply. Sticker fairs are another. As with any market, liquidity counts. The more people who can be attracted into the market with their duplicate cards, the better the chances of finding the sticker you want. Messrs Sardy and Velenik reckon that a group of ten people, swapping stickers efficiently and taking advantage of Panini's practice of selling the final 50 missing stickers to order, would need only 1,435 packs between them to complete all ten albums. Internet forums, where potentially unlimited numbers of people can swap stickers, mean that this number falls even further. The idea of a totally efficient market should dismay Panini, which would sell fewer packs as a result. Fortunately, as in all markets, behaviour is not strictly rational. Despite entreaties from parents and economists, younger football fans will always be prepared to tear out most of their stickers to get hold of Lionel Messi.

Do rent controls work?

The idea of allowing governments to set limits on the rents that can be charged by landlords strikes many people as a sensible way to address problems in housing markets. New York's mayor, Bill de Blasio, has campaigned vigorously for rent freezes on rent-stabilised apartments. In London, several mayoral hopefuls have mooted the idea of introducing some form of rent control to the city. Why are rent controls popular, and do they work?

Rent regulation can take various forms, including rent control (the placing of a cap on the rent that can be charged) and rent stabilisation (setting limits on how much rent can be raised over time). Supporters argue that introducing controls helps ensure that households on low and middle incomes are not squeezed out of cities in which housing costs are soaring. In many booming cities, growth has pushed up rents, and over time the composition of many neighbourhoods has changed in favour of those who can afford higher prices. Supporters of rent control often point to Germany, where it is illegal to charge rent more than 20% above the level charged for a comparable property. (Around 50% of people rent their housing in Germany; almost 90% of all Berliners do, many in pleasingly spacious, well-looked-after apartments.) In the ten years to 2014, the proportion of British households headed by someone aged between 25 and 34 which rented privately rose from 22% to 44%. In Seattle, rents for one-bedroom apartments increased by nearly 11% between 2010 and 2013. A case could be made that rent controls provide long-term security for renters, and tilt the balance of power away from landlords towards tenants. That, some reckon, makes for a fairer housing market, in which households with lower incomes cannot easily be pushed aside by landlords keen to "gentrify" the neighbourhood.

But economists, on both the left and the right, tend to disagree. As Paul Krugman wrote in the *New York Times* in 2000, rent control is "among the best-understood issues in all of economics, and – among economists, anyway – one of the least controversial".

Economists reckon a restrictive price ceiling reduces the supply of property to the market. When prices are capped, people have less incentive to fix up and rent out their basement flat, or to build rental property. Slower supply growth exacerbates the price crunch. And those landlords who do rent out their properties might not bother to maintain them, because when supply and turnover in the market are limited by rent caps, landlords have little incentive to compete to attract tenants. Rent controls also mean that landlords may also become choosier, and tenants may stay in properties longer than makes sense. And some evidence shows that those living in rent-controlled flats in New York tend to have higher median incomes than those who rent market-rate apartments. That may be because wealthier households may be in a better position to track down and secure rent-stabilised properties. The example of Germany is also an imperfect one: many cities there have seen declining populations and low (or falling) house prices over the past two decades, although the latter is now changing in several cities.

In places where demand for urban housing is rising (as in London, New York and Seattle), a more effective policy is simply to build more housing. The number of houses being built each year in Britain peaked in 1968 at 352,540 dwellings. Since 2008 there has been a particularly bad slump, while a restrictive "green belt" around the edges of London restricts growth. Meanwhile many developers sit on the land, watching its value grow. According to McKinsey, some 45% of land which is due to be developed in London remains idle. House-building rates are even lower in Germany, says Kath Scanlon of the London School of Economics. Restrictive zoning laws in places such as San Francisco (which also has rent control) could also be loosened, though locals might not like it. But in order to keep housing affordable, politicians will have to take on the NIMBYS, not just the landlords.

The economic case against minimum wages

Workers across the rich world have suffered stagnant wages for much of the past decade, in good times and bad. Governments are responding by proposing increases in minimum wage rates in America, Britain and Germany. A higher wage floor seems like a simple and sensible way to improve workers' fortunes. Yet many economists argue against it: Germany's leading economic institutes, for instance, have pushed Angela Merkel to resist calls for a wage floor. Why do economists often oppose minimum wages?

Historically, economists' scepticism was rooted in the worry that wage floors reduce employment. Firms will hire all the workers it makes sense to hire at prevailing wages, the thinking goes, so any minimum wage that forces firms to pay existing workers more will make those jobs uneconomical, leading to sackings. Yet economists were forced to rethink their views in the early 1990s, when David Card and Alan Krueger of America's National Bureau of Economic Research presented evidence that past minimum-wage increases had not had the expected effect on employment. A rise in New Jersey's minimum wage did not seem to slow hiring in fast-food restaurants in New Jersey relative to those in neighbouring Pennsylvania, they found. One explanation, some economists speculated, was that firms had previously been getting away with paying workers less than they were able, because workers were prevented from searching for better-paid work by the costs involved in changing jobs. That would mean that when wages were forced up, the firms were able to absorb the costs without firing anyone.

Academics continue to trade studies on whether minimum wages cost jobs. A 2013 survey of economists by the University of Chicago showed that a narrow majority of respondents believed that a rise in the US minimum wage to $9 per hour would make it "noticeably harder" for poor workers to find jobs. Yet a narrow majority also thought a rise would nonetheless be worthwhile, given the benefits to those who could find work. Economists' opposition to specific minimum-wage hikes is sometimes due to concerns that politicians will impose recklessly high wage floors, which firms may find difficult to absorb without laying people off. Some economists argue that there is a better alternative in the form of wage subsidies, which cost governments money but do not discourage hiring.

Recent minimum-wage debates have been complicated by the unusual macroeconomic circumstances of the day. When economies are plagued by weak demand, as much of the rich world has been since the financial crisis of 2007–08, firms may be more sensitive to wage floors. (Others argue that healthy corporate profits show that firms have plenty of room to accommodate pay rises.) New technologies could also amplify the employment effect of a wage hike. Given expanding opportunities for automation, firms may seize on higher wage floors as an excuse to reorganise production and shed jobs. But opinion among economists remains divided (and studies contradictory), because most recent minimum-wage increases have been comparatively modest. The argument over minimum wages seems set to run and run.

Who are the Pyongyangites of Pyonghattan?

Since Kim Jong-un came to power following the death of his father in December 2011, North Korea's Young Leader has shown a passion for construction projects, with the emphasis on leisure – something he promised his subjects early on, along with prosperity. Mr Kim swiftly ordered the renovation of the two main funfairs in the capital, Pyongyang. A new water park, 4D cinema, dolphinarium, riverside parks, residential skyscrapers and a new airport terminal all followed. And an underground shopping centre is being built in the capital to cater to a small class of newly monied Pyongyangites.

At the centre of this group sit the *donju*, wealthy traders whose investments have been fuelling a retail and construction boom in Pyongyang which is starting to change the face of the capital. A cluster of new high-rise apartments has been constructed, forming a quarter that local diplomats now refer to as "Pyonghattan". Successful *donju* own some of the foreign cars on the city's busier streets. Others ride in its expanding fleet of taxis. Most own smartphones. This growing segment of the population is already

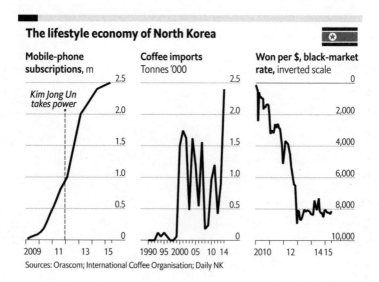

The lifestyle economy of North Korea

Mobile-phone subscriptions, m

Kim Jong Un takes power

2009 11 13 15

Coffee imports Tonnes '000

1990 95 2000 05 10 14

Won per $, black-market rate, inverted scale

2010 12 14 15

Sources: Orascom; International Coffee Organisation; Daily NK

visible on Pyongyang's streets as young women shrug off dowdy outfits in favour of fitted jackets, bolder colours and sunglasses. Coats with a discreet Burberry pattern on the lining are popular, and high heels have appeared, some in leopard print or silver. These goods have become more accessible with the gradual recognition of the market economy by the state. Reports even suggest that some workers have started to receive pay at black-market rates.

But for all the change in Pyongyang, this lifestyle remains within the reach only of a select few. Income inequality appears to be growing rapidly between those living in "Pyonghattan" and those in the city's shabbiest districts; between those who own cars and those who cannot yet afford a smartphone. But the starkest contrasts are with the North Korea beyond the capital, out in rural areas where men can be seen walking oxen through fields, and women washing their clothes in streams. To them and millions of others, Mr Kim's promises of a new era of prosperity and leisure must still sound hollow.

Why do so many Dutch people work part-time?

The Dutch are generally a pretty content bunch. The Netherlands consistently ranks as one of the best places in the world to live. Dutch kids are among the happiest in the world, according to Unicef. Some attribute their high quality of life and general good nature to a laid-back approach to work: more than half of the Dutch working population works part time, a far greater share than in any other rich-world country. On average only a fifth of the working-age population in EU member states holds a part-time job (8.7% of men and 32.2% of women); in the Netherlands 26.8% of men and 76.6% of women work less than 36 hours a week. Why?

Part of the reason is that Dutch women were relative latecomers to the labour market. Compared with other countries, few men had to leave to fight in the world wars of the 20th century, with the result that women did not labour in factories as they did in the US and Britain. Thanks to the country's wealth, a dual income was not a necessity for a comfortable life. And Dutch politics was dominated by Christian values until the 1980s: the focus was mainly on providing state aid (implicit subsidies in the fiscal system) so that women could stay at home with children.

This changed in the late 1980s, when the state realised that it would be a good idea to mobilise women into the workforce. But the cultural conviction that families still needed mothers to be home for tea-time prevailed, so the state worked closely with employers to ensure that the new part-time jobs would enjoy similar legal status to their full-time equivalents. This has, to an extent, continued: in 2000 the right for women and men to ask for a job to be part-time was written into law. But Ronald Dekker, a labour economist at Tilburg University, thinks this law is a confirmation of existing practice and therefore largely symbolic, only necessary for certain "archaic industries". Instead, he reckons, the high prevalence of part-time jobs is largely down to the wide availability of good-quality, well-paid "first tier" part-time jobs in the Netherlands: jobs often considered inferior in many other countries.

Whether part-time work is good for emancipation is questionable. Today, perhaps because part-time work is the norm, women in the Netherlands have a relatively high labour-force participation rate. But the Netherlands' record for getting women into top management roles is dire. The prevalence of part-time work seems to play a role: once you strip out part-timers, women make it into management roles nearly as often as men, according to the CBS (the main statistics agency in the Netherlands), although that doesn't include top management. The Dutch government has said that 30% of executive board positions should be held by women, but that may prove excessively optimistic; the level in 2015 was just 6%, according to Mijntje Luckerath, an academic at Tilburg University, who blames old-fashioned selection processes. And not all part-timers are pleased with their situation: before the financial crisis, fewer than 10% of Dutch part-timers wished they were employed full time; this has since risen to nearly 25%. That percentage is still much lower than in other EU countries, but it is a striking rise.

The thinking behind feminist economics

Economics, a discipline beloved by policy wonks, talking heads and *The Economist*, is meant to offer an objective way of looking at the world. But some worry that it falls short. Proponents of feminist economics believe that, in terms of both methodology and focus, economics is too much of a man's world. This is not just because women are under-represented in the science: in 2014, women constituted only 12% of American economics professors, and to date there has only been one female winner of the Nobel Memorial Prize in Economic Sciences (Elinor Ostrom). They also, perhaps more importantly, worry that by asking the wrong questions, economics has cemented gender inequality rather than helping to solve it. How do feminist economists want to change it?

According to Alfred Marshall, a founding father of the science, economics is "the study of men as they live and think and move in the ordinary business of life". Marshall's casual allusion to "men" captures what feminist economists believe is the first big problem with economics: a habit of ignoring women. The economy, they argue, is often thought of as the world of money, machines and men. This is reflected in how GDP is measured. Wage labour is included; unpaid work at home is not. Feminist economists criticise this approach as being excessively narrow. In Marilyn Waring's book *If Women Counted*, published in 1988, she argued that the system of measuring GDP was designed by men to keep women "in their place". Not only is this way of measuring GDP arbitrary (care is included in "production" when paid for on the market, but not when supplied informally), but because women contribute the bulk of care around the world, it also systematically undervalues their contribution to society. Dr Waring thought unpaid care should be included in GDP to reflect the fact that "production" of well-cared-for children is just as important as that of cars or crops.

When it comes to public policy, feminist economists think gender equality is valuable in and of itself, not just as a means of promoting growth. They also consider the effects of public policy on women. When public services are cut, a simple analysis might summarise the change in, say, the amount spent on employing civil servants. A feminist economist's analysis would probably point out that if those most likely to plug the gap left by the state are women, then this distribution of cuts could worsen gender inequality. And feminist economics also criticises the methods used within the standard models taught to undergraduates for overlooking fundamental drivers of gender inequality. Take a simple economics model, which might explain a woman's decision to take on the bulk of childcare responsibilities based on her preferences for "consumption" and "leisure". Feminist economists might point out that if her preferences have been formed by a society with strong ideas about what women should do, then presenting her choice as a free one could be misleading. By ignoring potential discrimination against women, such a model could allow sexism to go unchallenged, they would argue.

Proponents of feminist economics have won many battles. GDP might still not include unpaid care, but international agencies like the United Nations increasingly rely on broader measures of progress than cash income, including health and wellbeing. Julie Nelson, a feminist economist, writes in the *Journal of Economic Perspectives* that "many readers may have discovered that they are already doing 'feminist economics' in some ways, although they have preferred to think of themselves as just doing 'good economics'". Indeed, feminist economists wish they lived in a world where the label need not exist.

Why Swedish men take so much paternity leave

Along with its Nordic neighbours, Sweden features near the top of most gender-equality rankings. The World Economic Forum rates it as having one of the narrowest gender gaps in the world. But Sweden is not only a good place to be a woman: it also appears to be an idyll for new dads. Close to 90% of Swedish fathers take paternity leave. In 2013, some 340,000 dads took a total of 12 million days' leave, equivalent to about seven weeks each. Women take even more leave days to spend time with their children, but the gap is shrinking. Why do Swedish dads take so much time off work to raise their children?

Forty years ago Sweden became the first country in the world to introduce a gender-neutral paid parental-leave allowance. This involves paying 90% of wages for 180 days per child, and parents were free to divvy up the days between them in whatever way they pleased. But the policy was hardly a hit with dads: in the scheme's first year men took only 0.5% of all paid parental leave.

Now they take a quarter of it. One reason is that the scheme has become more generous, with the number of paid leave days for the first child being bumped up from 180 to 480. But it has also been tweaked to encourage a more equal sharing of the allowance. In 1995 the first so-called "daddy month" was introduced. Under this reform, families in which each parent took at least one month of leave received an additional month to add to their total allowance. The policy was expanded in 2002 so that if the mother and father each took at least two months' leave, the family would get two extra months. Some politicians now want to go further, proposing that the current system of shared leave be turned into one of individual entitlements, under which mothers should be allowed to take only half of the family's total allowance, with the rest reserved for fathers.

Policies similar to the Swedish "daddy months" have been introduced in other countries. Germany amended its parental-leave scheme in 2007 along Swedish lines, and within two years the share of fathers who took paid leave jumped from 3% to over 20%. One of the most powerful arguments in favour of splitting parental leave more equally is that it has positive ripple effects for women. After Swedish men started to take more responsibility for child-rearing, women have seen both their incomes and levels of self-reported happiness increase. Paying dads to change nappies and hang out at playgrounds, in other words, seems to benefit the whole family.

Which countries' citizens are best at managing their money?

Suppose you put $100 in a savings account that earns 10% interest each year. After five years, how much will you have? That was a question posed in a multiple-choice quiz (completed by 150,000 people in 144 countries) by the credit-rating agency Standard & Poor's. The answers proffered were "less than $150", "exactly $150" and "more than $150". The intention was to test whether respondents understood compound interest, in addition to basic mathematics (the correct answer is $161). Alas, not that many did: just one-third of them answered three out of five similar multiple-choice questions correctly. Scandinavians are the most financially literate: 70% were able to answer three questions correctly; the corresponding figure for Angolans and Albanians was 15%. While education plays a large role in determining financial literacy, the link with GDP per person is remarkably strong, too.

Previous research has shown that it can be difficult to convey financial know-how at a young age. Instead, it is gained through experience. In developed countries, knowledge follows a U-shaped curve, with middle-aged adults performing better in financial-literacy surveys than both the young and the old (who, through a combination of cognitive impairment and less education, do worse). In developing countries, financial literacy is better among the young, who have typically received more schooling.

The survey, the largest of its kind, demonstrates a striking gender divide in financial literacy. In 93 countries, the gap in correct answers between men and women was more than five percentage points. In Canada, 77% of men answered three questions correctly; the corresponding figure for women was just 60%. Women's lack of knowledge might well be explained by the deferring of financial decision-making to their husbands. But worryingly, the gender gap persists among well-educated single women too. When it comes to financial decision-making, many countries appear to be stuck in a 1960s time-warp.

It's a man's world
GDP and financial literacy

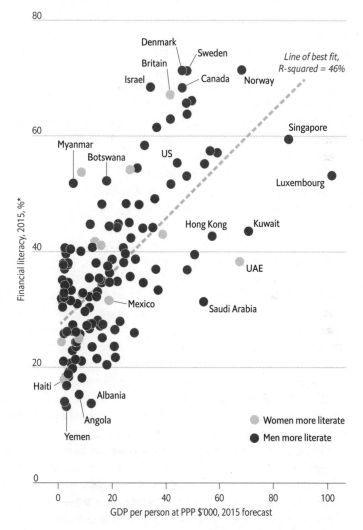

*Line of best fit,
R-squared = 46%*

Denmark
Sweden
Britain
Israel
Canada
Norway
Singapore
Myanmar
Botswana
US
Luxembourg
Hong Kong
Kuwait
UAE
Mexico
Saudi Arabia
Haiti
Albania
Angola
Yemen

Financial literacy, 2015, %*

80
60
40
20
0

Women more literate
Men more literate

GDP per person at PPP $'000, 2015 forecast

0   20   40   60   80   100

Sources: IMF; Standard & Poor's

*% of survey respondents answering three out
of four financial literacy questions correctly

Why the UN doesn't pay its interns

The story of an unpaid intern living in a tent in Geneva did not make the United Nations look good. David Hyde, a fresh-faced 22-year-old from New Zealand, said he set up camp on the banks of Lake Geneva because he could not afford the Swiss city's exorbitant rents while working without pay. The news stirred up public outrage as well as sympathy from Mr Hyde's colleagues: scores of UN interns in Geneva walked off the job on August 14th 2015 to protest against his plight. That same day a cluster of "interns' rights" groups penned an open letter to the UN's secretary-general, Ban Ki-moon, pointing out that the practice of not paying interns sits awkwardly with Article 23 of the organisation's own Universal Declaration of Human Rights ("Everyone who works has the right to just and favourable remuneration ensuring for himself and his family an existence worthy of human dignity"). So why doesn't the UN pay its interns?

The UN says that it would like to pay interns, but claims its hands are tied by a resolution passed in 1997 that forbids the payment of non-staff. Yet unpaid internships existed for decades before: a senior UN adviser recalls completing one in 1970 in New York. The resolution in fact simply acknowledged an old, ad hoc practice. But since the resolution, the UN's yearly intern intake has ballooned from 131 in 1996 to 4,018 in 2014. UN departments, unable to expand budgets and recruit staff, increasingly turn to an army of young graduates willing to work for free, for two to six months at a stretch. Though interns may protest, they clearly see value in the connections, experience and sense of purpose that UN internships provide, not to mention having its brand on their cvs.

If it wanted to pay its interns, the UN would struggle to find the money to do so. Paying 4,000 of them would cost up to €13 million ($14.5 million) per year – yet the UN has been cutting staff due to budget constraints. The fact that the US owes $1.3 billion in unpaid dues hardly helps. Internal resistance from clerical UN staff and their unions is another problem. They fear that paid internships may become a back door for recruitment and increase competition for coveted low-level "professional" positions. Others worry that a system of paid internships would be susceptible to nepotism: interns go through a much less rigorous – and less transparent – hiring process than that for official staff, which is governed by the UN Charter. Another barrier to paying interns is a larger matter regarding the geographical make-up of UN staff. The states that belong to the UN want to increase their influence by maximising their own citizens' presence among staff and vetoing measures that reduce it. Many developing countries regard paying interns, who are disproportionately from the wealthiest countries, as perpetuating injustice rather than correcting it (developed countries accounted for 61% of UN interns in 2007, despite having just 15% of the world's population). To fix that they may propose a geographical quota system for interns, which developed countries would oppose.

The UN may benefit from a policy of not paying interns, but it also suffers. Senior managers privately grumble about missing out on the best young talents, who accept paid offers elsewhere or cannot afford to live unpaid in swanky cities like Geneva and New York. The interns who can afford it, chiefly rich, metropolitan locals, fail to reflect the workplace diversity the UN strives to achieve. Back in Geneva, Mr Hyde has since packed up his tent and resigned, admitting the whole affair was a stunt to draw attention to the plight of unpaid workers. Those at the UN who push for change in his absence can take solace in the knowledge that the International Labour Organisation, a related body, began paying its interns a decade ago, after one of them was discovered living in the office basement. Others looking for paid work should note that there are plenty of organisations out there (including *The Economist*) that offer interns a decent wage.

Thomas Piketty's *Capital* summarised in four paragraphs

It is the economics book that took the world by storm. *Capital in the Twenty-First Century*, written by the French economist Thomas Piketty, was published in French in 2013 and in English in March 2014. The English version quickly became an unlikely bestseller, and it prompted a broad and energetic debate on the book's subject: the outlook for global inequality. Some reckon it heralds or may itself cause a pronounced shift in the focus of economic policy, toward distributional questions. *The Economist* hailed Professor Piketty as "the modern Marx" (Karl, that is). But what is his book all about?

Capital draws on more than a decade of research by Piketty and a handful of other economists, detailing historical changes in the concentration of income and wealth. This pile of data allows Piketty to sketch out the evolution of inequality since the beginning of the industrial revolution. In the 18th and 19th centuries western European society was highly unequal. Private wealth dwarfed national income and was concentrated in the hands of the rich families who sat atop a relatively rigid class structure. This system persisted even as industrialisation slowly contributed to rising wages for workers. Only the chaos of the first and second world wars and the Depression disrupted this pattern. High taxes, inflation, bankruptcies and the growth of sprawling welfare states caused wealth to shrink dramatically, and ushered in a period in which both income and wealth were distributed in relatively egalitarian fashion. But the shocks of the early 20th century have faded and wealth is now reasserting itself. On many measures, Piketty reckons, the importance of wealth in modern economies is approaching levels last seen before the first world war.

From this history, Piketty derives a grand theory of capital and inequality. As a general rule wealth grows faster than economic output, he explains, a concept he captures in the expression $r > g$ (where r is the rate of return to wealth and g is the economic growth rate). Other things being equal, faster economic growth will diminish the importance of wealth in a society, whereas slower growth will increase it (and demographic change that slows global growth will make capital more dominant). But there are no natural forces pushing against the steady concentration of wealth. Only a burst of rapid growth (from technological progress or rising population) or government intervention can be counted on to keep economies from returning to the "patrimonial capitalism" that worried Karl Marx. Piketty closes the book by recommending that governments step in now, by adopting a global tax on wealth, to prevent soaring inequality contributing to economic or political instability down the road.

The book has unsurprisingly attracted plenty of criticism. Some wonder whether Piketty is right to think that the future will look like the past. Theory argues that it should become ever harder to earn a good return on wealth the more there is of it. And today's super-rich (think of Bill Gates, or Mark Zuckerberg) mostly come by their wealth through their work, rather than via inheritance. Others argue that Piketty's policy recommendations are more ideologically than economically driven and could do more harm than good. But many of the sceptics nonetheless have kind words for the book's contributions, in terms of data and analysis. Whether or not Professor Piketty succeeds in changing policy, he will have influenced the way thousands of readers and plenty of economists think about these issues.

How airlines cut costs

In the 1980s a cabin crew at American Airlines observed that its passengers would happily wolf down in-flight dinner salads, but nearly three-quarters of them would leave the customary olive. Robert Crandall, the company's boss at the time, promptly removed it. It turned out that the airline paid its caterers based on the number of ingredients in the salad: 60 cents for four items and 80 cents for five. The olive was the fifth item. This move saved more than $40,000 a year. In 1994, Southwest Airlines followed the suggestion of a flight attendant and removed the company's logo from rubbish bags, saving the carrier $300,000 a year in printing costs. In an industry that serves fussy customers and operates on thin margins, how else do modern airlines cut costs without cutting corners?

They start by mimicking doughnut-dodging supermodels who watch their weight down to the second decimal place. Airlines bin bulky in-flight magazines, lay thinner carpets and serve food in light cardboard boxes. Some airlines have jettisoned safety equipment for emergency water landings on those aircraft that do not fly above water. Seats have become lighter. In its Airbus A321 planes, Air Méditerranée, a French carrier, replaced 220 economy seats, each weighing 12kg, with skinnier ones made from lighter materials such as titanium that weigh around 4kg. GoAir, an Indian low-cost carrier, hires only female flight attendants because they are on average 10–15kg lighter than men. Such parsimony pays off. Fuel accounts for a third of an airline's costs and every kilogram thus shed removes $100 from an aircraft's annual fuel bill.

Small design tweaks on modern aircraft, which are not as thirsty as their predecessors, also help. Southwest Airlines estimates that it saves 54 million gallons of fuel a year after installing winglets, or upturned wingtips, on its fleet to reduce drag. EasyJet, a European budget carrier, uses special paint that eliminates microscopic bumps on the aircraft's body to help it cut through air more easily and, the airline claims, burn less fuel. Internationally, pilots are being persuaded not take off at full throttle and to get their aircraft to cruising altitude (where the air is thinner and there is less drag) as quickly as possible. When landing on long runways, pilots may let the aircraft slow down on its own instead of putting the engines into reverse thrust. Some low-cost carriers like India's SpiceJet have learned to work their fleet aggressively. Pilots of its Bombardier Q400 turboprops, which serve smaller cities, fly their planes faster to shave a few minutes of flight-time off each leg, which lets the airline squeeze in an additional flight every day. The increased fuel burn at higher speeds is more than paid for by the additional revenue from the extra flight.

And yet for all the stress that airlines willingly take on, boarding delays cost them up to $1 billion a year in Europe alone. Airbus thinks it has the answer: it has been granted a patent for a portable cabin that copies the seating arrangement of an aircraft. The module, docked at a gate, is loaded with passengers and their luggage and is then slotted into an empty aircraft like a matchbox that neatly slips into its case. The plane then flies to its destination; after landing the detachable cabin is removed and replaced by another module containing a new set of passengers ready for take-off. The futuristic design seems likely to cost billions of dollars and many years to develop – and it may never get off the ground. In the meantime, airlines will continue to weed out that extra olive.

Why private schooling is on the decline in England

England's private schools are struggling to attract pupils. Although the number of school-age children has risen since 2008, the number attending independent schools has barely grown. As a result, the proportion of children at such schools has slipped from 7.2% to 6.9%, with absolute numbers falling everywhere apart from the prosperous south-east. Why are English parents – a famously pushy bunch – becoming more reluctant to pay for their children's education?

Much is down to cost. One study found that fees had gone up by around 20% between 2010 and 2015. As a result, the average price of a year's education at a boarding school is now more than £30,000 ($45,000); a day place costs around half that. Evidently boarding schools are no longer renowned for their Spartan conditions (one

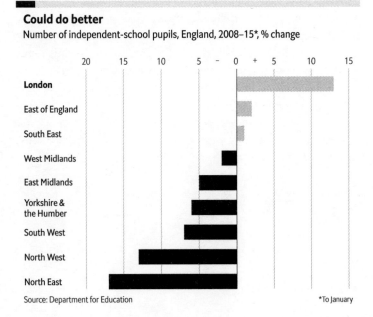

Could do better
Number of independent-school pupils, England, 2008–15*, % change

Source: Department for Education   *To January

even provides televisions and games consoles in students' rooms). But this has also pushed the price of a private education beyond the means of many professionals, particularly those with more than one child. Meanwhile, improving state schools – and a decline in snobbery – make the alternative increasingly attractive.

The fall in numbers is largely confined to the lower end of the market, however. In his book *The Old Boys: The Decline and Rise of the Public School* (2015), David Turner claims this is a golden age for Britain's grandest private schools, with standards of care, facilities and education higher than ever before. As a result, they are able to attract pupils from around the world. And some have even established branches in far-flung places such as Kazakhstan and Qatar. But smaller provincial schools, particularly those beyond the reach of London's airports, are a less appealing proposition to those from abroad. Some have closed, others have merged and many more have simply focused on teaching fewer pupils for more money. Intriguingly, at least 19 private schools have entered the state sector as academies (which have greater freedom from government regulation than ordinary state schools, but are still free to attend).

The declining popularity of private education is not just an English phenomenon: parents in America are also turning away from fee-paying schools. In both countries, the result is more pressure on state resources. And falling private-school attendance is likely to be one reason why the well-off are grabbing an ever-larger share of government spending. The decline of private schools – long desired by many on the left – could turn out to have tricky and unwelcome consequences.

Also on the menu: leisure and pleasure

Why Guinness is less Irish than you think

St Patrick's Day, on March 17th, is an annual celebration of all things Irish – and of one thing in particular. Around Ireland, and all over the world, people celebrate with a pint or two (or three, or four) of Guinness, Ireland's unofficial national intoxicant. Publicans love St Patrick's Day, so much so that it can sometimes feel like less a celebration of Irish culture than a marketing event for Guinness's owner, Diageo. Now exported to more than 120 countries, the black stuff has become a powerful symbol of Ireland. But how Irish is it really?

Arthur Guinness, who founded a brewery in Dublin in 1759, might have been surprised that his drink would one day become such a potent national symbol. He was a committed unionist and opponent of Irish nationalism; before the Irish Rebellion of 1798 he was even accused of spying for the British authorities. His descendants continued to support unionism passionately – in 1913, one gave the Ulster Volunteer Force £10,000 (worth about £1 million, or $1.4 million, in today's money) to fund a paramilitary campaign to resist Ireland being given legislative independence. The company was alleged to have lent men and equipment to the British army to help crush Irish rebels during the Easter Rising of 1916, afterwards firing members of staff whom it believed to have Irish-nationalist sympathies.

The beer the company has become most famous for – porter stout – was based on a London ale, a favourite of the street porters of Covent Garden and Billingsgate markets. Since 1886 the firm's shares have been traded on the London Stock Exchange, and the company moved its headquarters to London in 1932, where it has been based ever since (it merged with Grand Metropolitan and renamed itself Diageo in 1997). As recently as the 1980s, the company has even considered disassociating itself from its Irish heritage. Worried about the impact on sales of the IRA's terrorist campaign during the Troubles, Guinness came close in 1982 to relaunching the brand as an English beer brewed in west London. But as Northern

Ireland's situation improved in the 1990s, the company's marketing strategy changed again towards marketing the beer as Irish, aiming its product at tourists in Ireland and the estimated 70 million people of Irish descent living around the world. Now the Guinness Storehouse, part of the original Dublin factory which was reopened as a tourist attraction in 2000, promotes Guinness to tourists as an Irish beer once again.

Guinness is not the only company to play up or hide its national origins in an effort to boost sales. Jacob's biscuits have been marketed by some shops as being British, in spite of the company's origins as an Irish company from Waterford. And Lipton now markets its black tea on the strength of the company's British origins, in over 100 countries – except Britain, where it is not widely sold. In a world where multinational companies control a large chunk of the global food supply chain, national identity – at least in branding – matters as much as ever.

Booze, bonks and bodies

Box-office Bond
Average per James Bond film of:

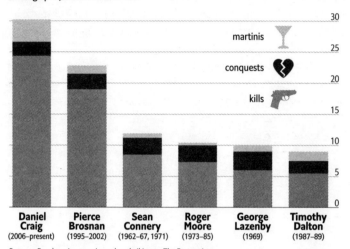

Sources: Bondmovies.com; jamesbondwiki.com; *The Economist*

Ah, my dear fellow... so we meet again. *Spectre*, the 24th James Bond film, was released in October 2015. Its mission: to draw even more fans to the newly revitalised franchise. The previous instalment, *Skyfall* (2012), was the most successful Bond film to date, surpassing *Thunderball* (1965). Much has stayed the same over the years, from bow ties and baccarat to Aston Martins and the Walther PPK – and, of course, those martinis. But crunching the numbers reveals that latter-day Bonds have prospered by placing a greater emphasis on kills rather than conquests, and toning down the sexism of earlier films. Daniel Craig, the sixth on-screen 007, has been the most successful: his films have taken an average of £800 million ($1.2 billion) at the box office (though the first three Bond movies grossed more than 30 times their production costs, compared with just four times for the three most recent).

But with Mr Craig now said to be handing in his licence to kill, where will the franchise go next? While choosing his replacement, the producers should take a close look at the data: it seems that audiences prefer action in the field to antics in the bedroom. So do not be surprised if James Bond goes further in the direction of another action hero: Jason Bourne. While keeping his bow tie on, of course.

Why people like pizza in hard times

The fast food business has seen better days. In 2014, annual global revenue at McDonald's fell for the first time in 12 years, prompting the burger chain to appoint a new chief executive to turn things around. As consumers become more health-conscious, cheap fast food seems to be losing its appeal. But there is a striking exception to this downward trend. Even as they buy fewer takeaway burgers, people seem to have a growing appetite for pizza, from both independent pizzerias and pizza chains. As revenues at McDonald's have fallen, for example, those at Domino's Pizza have continued to rise: in March 2016, the pizza chain reported strong domestic sales for the last three months of 2015, and its 88th consecutive quarter of growth in same-store sales growth for its international division. What accounts for the growing popularity of pizza?

Pizza has long been a favoured form of inexpensive fast food in Italy, where people started putting tomato on flatbread some time in the 18th century. In the early 20th century, Italian immigrants popularised pizza in America. Demand boomed after the second world war thanks to returning American soldiers, who had gained a taste for pizza in Italy.

Today, pizza is benefiting from the trend towards healthy cooking – though it is not entirely clear that it deserves to. People assume that pizza, with fresh toppings including vegetables, must be healthier than a burger. (In fact, a medium-sized vegetarian pizza can contain as much as four times as many calories as a Big Mac.) Pizza has also benefited as consumers reined in their spending after the financial crisis; ordering a pizza delivery is cheaper than going out to eat, so pizzerias have benefitted as people have traded down from going to restaurants. And as economies have recovered after the crisis, takeaways have stayed popular as household budgets remain squeezed.

But the secret ingredient that keeps consumers hooked on pizza is menu innovation. Pizza chains are constantly coming up with alluring (and, in some cases, disgusting) new variations of their product to maintain consumers' interest and loyalty, such as pizzas with crusts stuffed with bacon and cheese, pizzas with a rim of tear-off, cheese-stuffed garlic bread, and even pizzas with tiny cheeseburgers around the edge. Cleverer still, these novelty pizzas are difficult to cook at home. No wonder pizza accounts for a growing slice of fast-food consumption.

Why women's sport is less popular than men's

A few hours before the men's Tour de France arrived in Paris on July 27th 2014, a group (or peloton) of women cyclists dashed up the Champs Elysées. It was the inaugural race of La Course, a one-day event organised by the people behind the Tour de France, and the latest attempt to launch a women's version of the main competition. Previous efforts have foundered because of a lack of interest among sponsors and the public. The difficulty of creating a women's Tour illustrates a wider phenomenon: with a few exceptions, professional women's sport is much less popular than the male equivalent. Why?

If there were more sponsorship and media coverage, some say, then women's sport would be more popular. Media outlets and sponsors retort that if women's sport attracted more interest in the first place then they would invest more time and money in it. All sides agree on what it takes to make a sport successful: a balance of consumer, media and commercial appeal.

Sponsors are unwilling to finance individuals and teams that don't get good exposure – and few female athletes do. The Women's Sport and Fitness Foundation (WSFF) estimates that in 2013, women's sports received 7% of coverage and 0.4% of the total value of commercial sponsorships. This is a vicious circle: viewers want to watch sports at the highest professional standard, and sponsors want to be associated with the best athletes. Because of the lack of sponsorship many female athletes, even those who represent their countries, have to fit training around employment. Those who are paid usually earn less than male colleagues. The Professional Golfers' Association, for instance, offers $256 million in prize money; the women's association offers only $50 million. This inequality is echoed in pay for coaches for women's teams.

Things are changing. The English women's cricket team became professional in 2014, signing a two-year sponsorship deal with carmaker Kia after winning back-to-back Ashes contests. Wimbledon, the oldest tennis tournament, started awarding women the same amount of prize money as men in 2007, and the prize money for the winner of La Course is equivalent to that for a stage winner in Le Tour. Other sports are being leaned on to follow suit. More strikingly, the opinions of sports fans seem to be shifting: 61% of fans surveyed by the WSFF said they believed top sportswomen were just as skilful as their male equivalents and over half said women's sport was just as exciting to watch.

This will matter more when, as seems likely, the increasing numbers of women participating in regular sport yield more potential pros. In Britain, 750,000 adults took up team sports after the 2012 Olympics; 500,000 of them were women. More female participants and viewers should encourage sponsors and the media to balance their coverage. Until then, athletes could consider taking a leaf out of Marie Marvingt's book. In 1908, when she was denied the right to ride in the Tour de France because she was a woman, she ignored the rules and raced anyway, 15 minutes behind the men. Of the 115 people who started the 4,488km (2,789 mile) race that year, only 37 managed to complete it: 36 men and one woman.

Why eating insects makes sense

The world's population is projected to reach 11 billion by the end of the 21st century. Feeding that many people will be a challenge, which is further complicated by the impact of climate change on agriculture. That is why some people advocate an unusual way to boost the food supply and feed people sustainably: by eating less meat, and more insects.

About 2 billion people already eat bugs. Mexicans enjoy chili-toasted grasshoppers. Thais tuck into cricket stir-fries and Ghanaians snack on termites. Insects are slowly creeping onto Western menus as novelty items, but most people remain squeamish. Yet there are three reasons why eating insects makes sense.

First, they are healthier than meat. There are nearly 2,000 kinds of edible insects, many of them packed with protein, calcium, fibre, iron and zinc. A small serving of grasshoppers can contain about the same amount of protein as a similar sized serving of beef, but has far less fat and far fewer calories. Second, raising insects is cheap, or free. Little technology or investment is needed to produce them. Harvesting insects could provide livelihoods to some of the world's poorest people. Finally, insects are a far more sustainable source of food than livestock. Livestock production accounts for nearly a fifth of all greenhouse-gas emissions – more than transport. By contrast, insects produce relatively few greenhouse gases, and raising them requires much less land and water. And they'll eat almost anything.

Despite all this, most Westerners find insects hard to swallow. One solution is to use protein extracted from bugs in other products, such as ready meals and pasta sauces. Not having to look at the bugs, and emphasising the environmental benefits, might be the best way to make the idea of eating insects a bit more palatable.

A graphical history of Disney films

Walt Disney was a textbook example of a polymath: he was an innovator, entrepreneur, cartoonist, voice actor, animator, studio boss, theme park creator/owner and film producer. The company he started (from a cartoon studio set up with his brother Roy in 1923) grew in line with his ambition to reflect his disparate array of talents. An animator first and foremost, Walt created and licensed Mortimer (later Mickey) Mouse in response to losing the rights to his first character, Oswald the Lucky Rabbit. Mickey appeared in a series of short animations, including Disney's first venture into sound: *Steamboat Willie*, voiced by Walt himself. Other popular characters followed, as did the world's first full-colour commercial cartoon in 1930 before the Walt Disney Company moved on to more ambitious animated feature films. *Snow White and the Seven Dwarfs* in 1937 began an incredibly prolific period spawning the classics *Pinocchio* and *Fantasia* (1940), *Dumbo* (1941) and *Bambi* (1942). The company diversified further in the 1950s, opening the original Disneyland theme park in California.

An intricate flowchart drawn by Walt in 1957 elegantly lays out the firm's component parts and strategy, with films at the centre surrounded by theme parks, merchandise, music, publishing and television. It shows how each part provides content and drives sales for the others. After Walt's death at 65 in 1966, however, the company began to stray from his original model. Disney's animated output underwent a fallow period, greatly outnumbered by live action titles (only twelve fully-animated features were produced from the 1960s to the late 1980s) and the company plugged the gap by reissuing former triumphs such as *Cinderella* and *Lady and the Tramp* during the 1980s.

Disney didn't sit still for long, however, adding to its empire in the 1980s and 1990s with TV channels (the Disney Channel, ABC/ESPN) and retail stores (the company has always had a firm grasp of the value of merchandising). But by the 2000s it seemed the formerly famous innovative flair of Disney was on ice. Its

From *Fantasia* to *Frozen*
The history and share price of The Walt Disney Company

Selected film releases

Disney Park openings

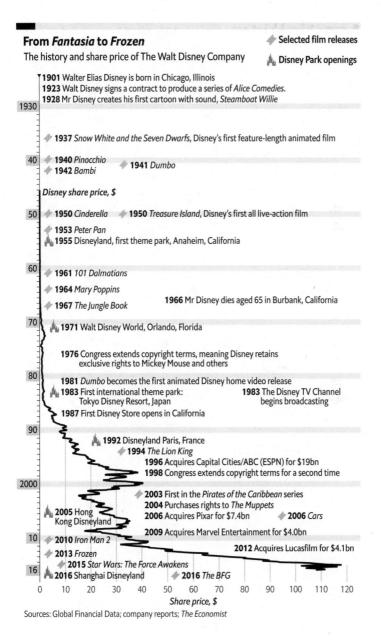

1901 Walter Elias Disney is born in Chicago, Illinois
1923 Walt Disney signs a contract to produce a series of *Alice Comedies*.
1928 Mr Disney creates his first cartoon with sound, *Steamboat Willie*

1930

1937 *Snow White and the Seven Dwarfs*, Disney's first feature-length animated film

40 **1940** *Pinocchio*   **1941** *Dumbo*
    1942 *Bambi*

Disney share price, $

50 **1950** *Cinderella*   **1950** *Treasure Island*, Disney's first all live-action film

    1953 *Peter Pan*
    1955 Disneyland, first theme park, Anaheim, California

60 **1961** *101 Dalmatians*

    1964 *Mary Poppins*
                              1966 Mr Disney dies aged 65 in Burbank, California
    1967 *The Jungle Book*

70 **1971** Walt Disney World, Orlando, Florida

    1976 Congress extends copyright terms, meaning Disney retains
             exclusive rights to Mickey Mouse and others

80 **1981** *Dumbo* becomes the first animated Disney home video release
    1983 First international theme park: **1983** The Disney TV Channel
             Tokyo Disney Resort, Japan   begins broadcasting
    1987 First Disney Store opens in California

90 **1992** Disneyland Paris, France
    1994 *The Lion King*
             1996 Acquires Capital Cities/ABC (ESPN) for $19bn
             1998 Congress extends copyright terms for a second time

2000
             2003 First in the *Pirates of the Caribbean* series
             2004 Purchases rights to *The Muppets*
    2005 Hong   **2006** Acquires Pixar for $7.4bn   **2006** *Cars*
    Kong Disneyland
             2009 Acquires Marvel Entertainment for $4.0bn

10 **2010** *Iron Man 2*
                                          2012 Acquires Lucasfilm for $4.1bn
    2013 *Frozen*
    2015 *Star Wars: The Force Awakens*
16 **2016** Shanghai Disneyland   **2016** *The BFG*

    0   10   20   30   40   50   60   70   80   90   100 110 120
                              Share price, $

Sources: Global Financial Data; company reports; *The Economist*

animation unit stagnated after the departure in 1994 of its studio chief, Jeffrey Katzenberg. The most successful animated films Disney released during this time were computer-drawn pictures made for the company by Pixar, beginning with *Toy Story* in 1995. Meanwhile DreamWorks SKG, co-founded by Mr Katzenberg, began making hit computer-generated animation films as well, including the blockbuster *Shrek* franchise. Unaccustomed to playing second fiddle, Disney appointed a new chief executive with a strong vision in 2005: Bob Iger. He set about reviving founder Walt Disney's original formula on an even more ambitious scale, putting films back at the heart of the business. A series of shrewd acquisitions followed Iger's appointment. He cannily revitalised Disney's own film-making brand by buying Pixar in 2006 and Marvel Entertainment, stable of the *Avengers* franchise (*Iron Man*, *The Hulk* et al.), in 2009.

It then bought Lucasfilm for $4.1 billion in 2012, gaining control of the lucrative *Star Wars* franchise (with the added benefit of all the merchandising and toy sales that come with it). The release of the *The Force Awakens* in 2015 represented more than just the revival of a beloved science-fiction series. It was an example of the way Disney has prospered over the past decade to become the envy of the entertainment industry. Profits have more than doubled in the past five years, to $8.4 billion, and Disney's share price has risen nearly fivefold over the past ten, easily beating its rivals Comcast, 21st Century Fox, Time Warner and Viacom. Disney is the most valuable of the lot, worth a star-studded $186 billion.

How India Pale Ale conquered the world

India Pale Ale (IPA) once had a good claim to be the first global beer, before lager took a grip on the world's tipplers. Now IPA, an amber, hop-laden brew, high in alcohol, is regaining its global footprint. Arguments rage about the origins and history of IPA. Britain's territories on the Indian subcontinent were generally too hot for brewing. So a couple of hundred years ago, to keep army officers and officials of the East India Company away from the fearsome local firewater, beer was exported from Britain to take its place. Whether a beer already existed that had the characteristics of IPA or whether it was developed for the purpose is a matter of heated debate among beer historians. What is clear is that hops, which act as a preservative as well as a flavouring, combined with a hefty dose of alcohol for added robustness, ensured that the beer survived the long sea journey to India. Indeed, the months jiggling in a barrel onboard seemed only to improve the flavour. The style caught on at home, as the brew seeped onto the domestic market.

IPA's popularity waned as the brewing industry changed. After the second world war, big brewers in Britain and America bought smaller competitors and flooded the market with bland, mass-market beers as old styles were abandoned in favour of a pint that would not offend anyone. But in the 1980s brewing began to change again. The craft-beer revolution, which started in the US, was a reaction to the domination of the market by these dull and flavourless brews. Small beermakers, encouraged by tax breaks and an urge to drink a beer with some character, began to produce small batches of more adventurous ales. The taste for these beers caught on. The result is that the US is now home to more than 2,500 breweries, compared with about 50 in the 1970s. Beer drinking is in overall decline as wealthy boozers switch to wine and spirits, but craft beer is growing fast, as consumers turn against the mass market to savour more expensive and exclusive brews.

The beer that craft brewers like making the most is IPA. Artisan beermakers in the US adopted old recipes from Britain for their

IPAs but gradually began to adapt the brews to their own tastes. The heavy use of hops allows them to show off their skills in blending different flavours. Some parts of the US have, like Britain, an excellent climate for growing top-quality hops. The bold flavours and high alcohol content create a beer that has a distinct style and bold taste, yet can come in many shades. The passion for hops in US craft beers has taken on the characteristics of an arms race, as brewers try to outdo each other in hoppiness. (Many bottles now list their score in international bitterness units, or IBU, as a badge of pride.)

If no brewer in the US can pass up the opportunity to make an IPA, the same is true elsewhere. As the craft-beer revolution has spread beyond America, so has the taste for IPA. Britain is undergoing a brewing revival alongside a foodie revolution, based on local produce and artisanal methods. Much the same is happening in other rich countries around the world, where breweries are springing up to produce craft beers. Indeed, IPA has come full circle. Many British craft brewers are using new IPA recipes imported from the US for their brews, but again adapting them for local palates. IPA may not yet have displaced lager as the global tipple, but it is at least battling for bar space with mainstream beers. Who could feel bitter about that?

Why doping in sport is so hard to catch

For more than two decades, 50 was a kind of magic figure for cyclists in the Tour de France. That is the maximum threshold for hematocrit, the percentage of oxygen-carrying red-blood cells that can be found coursing through human vessels without external help. In *The Secret Race*, Tyler Hamilton, a former cyclist for the American team, likened the number to his personal stock price ("You are 43," his doctor told him). Britain's David Millar called it "the cyclist's holy grail". Breach the 50-mark and be suspended on the reasonable suspicion that you were using EPOs (erythropoietins), which boost red-blood cell production; but ride with a lower figure and risk being left behind. Of all top-ten finishes in the Tour de France from 1998 to 2013, 38% were found to have doped themselves with EPOs. Another analysis of 12,000 track-and-field athletes' leaked blood results, released in 2014, suggested that 800 of them, or 6%, were "highly suggestive of doping". Yet each year only 1–2% of all tests result in penalties. Why is doping in sport so hard to catch?

Doping, as old as sport itself, derives from the Dutch word *doop*, an opium stimulant consumed by ancient Greeks. Raucous crowds would come to see juiced-up athletes have a Greco-Roman go at each other. Their enthusiasm would endure and evolve. In 1889, when James "Pud" Galvin, an American baseball player, got merrily soused with a concoction made from monkey's testicles and had a dream run, the *Washington Post* lauded it as "the best proof yet furnished of the value of the discovery" of a new drug's virtue. At the start of the 20th century, chemicals like cocaine, ether and amphetamines became popular among athletes. Most of these drugs targeted the brain and reduced fatigue; later, steroids and corticoids helped build muscles. It was during the cold war, in the 1970s, that drug use escalated into a full-blown crisis. Members of the Warsaw Pact encouraged "systematic doping" of their female athletes, "often without their knowledge", writes David Epstein in *The Sports Gene*. Of the top 80 women's shot-puts of all time, for instance, 75 were thrown between the mid-1970s and 1990. It was a time when women gained rapidly on men in track-and-field events; doctors had discovered they could boost their performance simply by injecting them with testosterone.

It was never good for the athletes' health, but today doping like that carries the more immediate risk of detection and disqualification. The preferred method today is therefore "micro-dosing". Instead of injecting EPO subcutaneously (under the skin), risking a longer "glow time" during which they might be found out, athletes have learned to administer smaller doses directly into their veins. Marginal gains matter. The difference between the first and second place in the 100m dash may be just 0.01 seconds, faster than the blink of an eye. It doesn't help that some athletes have natural genetic mutations that give them a legitimate advantage over their peers. This quirk of biology happens to make life easier for dopers, too. The most common anti-doping test is called a T/E ratio, where "T" stands for testosterone and "E" is a steroid called epitestosterone. The human body normally has equal amounts of "T" and "E" in the blood. But the World Anti-Doping Agency (WADA) allows T/E ratios as high as 4:1, to allow for the small segment of the population who have the natural genetic variation. Hence, the ordinary-blooded athlete finds wiggle room to dope, at least until he brushes up against T/E 4:1.

To address some of these issues, the "Athlete Biological Passport" (ABP) was introduced in 2009. The passport records all of an athlete's vital physiological records to generate a baseline blood profile. Over time, an electronic trail should allow testers to see unnatural variations and sudden spikes to compare against the body's natural ability to, say, produce red-blood cells or burn lactic acid. So far the tool appears to have worked as a deterrent. Until recently, there was no test to detect "blood doping", a method of transfusing samples of one's own refrigerated blood back into the body, to increase the red-blood-cell count. But the ABP should be smart enough to pick up on such anomalies. Since it was implemented, the percentage of tests hinting at an unusual increase in red-blood-cell count has fallen by half: a small but significant start. Clever drugs and even cleverer ways of administering them will continue to evade testers until anti-doping agencies receive more funding (WADA's budget is just $30 million) and there is less corruption (tip-offs before random out-of-competition drug tests are common). Where doping is concerned, the arms race has outrun the cold war.

The careers of the original *Star Wars* cast

A long time ago, the three actors who portrayed the primary "human" characters in the original *Star Wars* trilogy – Mark Hamill (Luke Skywalker), Carrie Fisher (Princess Leia) and Harrison Ford (Han Solo) – went into their roles as relative unknowns, but emerged as superstars. Having not starred together since, they were reunited in the *The Force Awakens*, the revival of the franchise by Walt Disney Studios in 2015.

Over the decades since the original films, the careers of the three stars could hardly have contrasted more. Mr Hamill and Ms Fisher have enjoyed few screen successes between them, though the latter found a career as a bestselling author and Hollywood script-doctor. Mr Hamill, meanwhile, fronted some notable turkeys, including *Watchers Reborn* (1998), a straight-to-video effort centred around a secret government experiment, a mutant killer beast, and a dog with an IQ of 140. For some of the *Star Wars* stars, the enormous popularity of the films and their larger-than-life characters meant fans were unable to associate them with other roles. Sir Alec Guinness, the veteran stage and screen actor who starred alongside them in the first of the series, came to resent the association with his character Obi-Wan Kenobi so much that he immediately binned all fan mail, unopened.

The only one of the major characters unable to use *the Force* perhaps took advantage of the force of his own charisma. Mr Ford went from playing Han Solo to embody the equally swashbuckling hero Indiana Jones in *Raiders of the Lost Ark* (1981), and then Rick Deckard, the replicant-hunting antihero of *Blade Runner* (1982). Achieving recognition in other imaginary universes before typecasting had fully set in may have helped – his first appearances as "Indy" and Deckard fell between the *Star Wars* titles. Yet not even Mr Ford's successes have come halfway to matching the box-office returns of the 1977 film that started it all.

A new, new hope?

Film careers of the primary cast of the original *Star Wars* trilogy, 1977–2015

US gross box office, \$bn* 0.5 ○ ○ ◯ ◯ 1.5 • no data

 A New Hope (1977)

 The Empire Strikes Back (1980)

 Return of the Jedi (1983)

 The Force Awakens (2015)

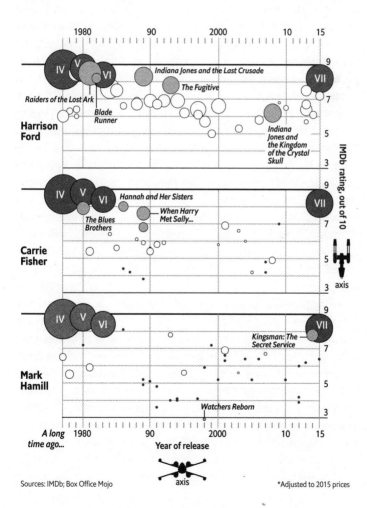

Harrison Ford — Raiders of the Lost Ark, Blade Runner, Indiana Jones and the Last Crusade, The Fugitive, Indiana Jones and the Kingdom of the Crystal Skull

Carrie Fisher — The Blues Brothers, Hannah and Her Sisters, When Harry Met Sally...

Mark Hamill — Watchers Reborn, Kingsman: The Secret Service

IMDb rating, out of 10

axis

A long time ago... Year of release

axis

Sources: IMDb; Box Office Mojo

*Adjusted to 2015 prices

How professional sportsmen observe Ramadan

In 2014, Ramadan began on June 28th, just as the knockout stage of matches in the football World Cup got under way in Brazil. It was the first time since 1986 that the tournament had coincided with Islam's holy month. That caused a dilemma for some Muslim footballers. During Ramadan observant Muslims are expected to refrain from eating, drinking and sex, from dawn until sunset. Contrary to their licentious reputation, most players can cope with the last. Nutrition, though, is considered critical to a sportsman's preparation – particularly in Brazil, where the climate can be punishing for even the best-prepared athletes. In Fortaleza, which hosted several big games, daylight lasts around 12 hours, with the sun rising and setting at around 5.30am and 5.30pm. The average maximum temperature in July is 30°C (86°F); humidity reaches an average of 92%. So how do footballers who observe Ramadan cope?

Many teams in the 2014 World Cup had a large Muslim presence – and not only those representing predominantly Islamic countries such as Bosnia & Herzegovina, Algeria and Iran. Star players from France (Karim Benzema), Germany (Mesut Özil), Switzerland (Philippe Senderos), Belgium (Marouane Fellaini) and Ivory Coast (Yaya Touré), among numerous others, had to decide how to deal with Ramadan, in case their teams made it that far in the competition.

Players are advised to eat plenty of slow-release carbohydrates, like sweet potato and corn, outside fasting hours, according to Zaf Iqbal, Liverpool FC's club doctor. They should also avoid anything with too much sugar, which is a quick-release carbohydrate. However, sports nutritionists suggest that the lack of fluid has a bigger impact than the lack of food. Dehydration can affect cognitive functions. Muslim athletes often report feeling fatigued and can suffer from mood swings during Ramadan, according to a 2009 paper in the *International Journal of Sports Physiology and Performance*. It can also increase the risk of injury. Muslim footballers are told to drink plenty of liquid before dawn, and to make sure they do not train during the hottest parts of the day. Indeed, as fasting can also affect sleep patterns, some team doctors advise players to take a siesta instead. When such steps are taken, most studies suggest that athletes' training performance is not adversely affected.

But dehydration during matches can be a problem. Unlike training sessions, match times cannot be tailored to a sportsman's needs. So many Muslim athletes take a pragmatic approach. While some, such as Kolo Touré, an Ivory Coast defender, are strict observers, others, like Marouane Chamakh, a forward for Morocco (which did not qualify), fast on most days but not on the eve of a game or on matchday itself. Others postpone fasting altogether during important events. During the London Olympics in 2012, which also coincided with Ramadan, Abdul Buhari, a British shot-putter, told the *Guardian* he believed it was impossible to stay in peak condition while fasting, so he came to another arrangement: "I believe God is forgiving, and I'll make up for every single day I've missed."

David Bowie's genre-hopping career

Some called him a chameleon, but David Bowie was the reverse. Chameleons change hue to blend in with their background; he changed to stand out, and dared others to mimic him. He was never afraid to murder his darlings. Ziggy Stardust, his most famous alter-ego, was killed off in 1973 as he finished an exhausting worldwide tour at London's Hammersmith Odeon; he was being too much imitated, and Bowie always had to be one step ahead. One successor was Aladdin Sane, a zigzag of painted lightning across his face; another, the most troubled, was the Thin White Duke, an aristocratic cabaret singer in black trousers, waistcoat and white shirt, needing only a skull to play Hamlet. Over the course of his career Bowie explored an extraordinary range of genres and styles and worked with a wide range of collaborators – yet, amid all the changes, he always managed to sound just like himself.

Changes
The careers of David Bowie

Key collaborations	Studio albums	Genres

BERLIN | LA | LONDON

Tony Visconti
Mick Ronson
Rick Wakeman

Lou Reed

John Lennon
Brian Eno
Iggy Pop
Robert Fripp
Carlos Alomar

Queen
Bing Crosby
Nile Rodgers
Stevie Ray Vaughan
Mick Jagger

NEW YORK

Pet Shop Boys
Trent Reznor
Goldie

Massive
Attack

Scarlett
Johansson

Arcade Fire

Studio albums

DAVID BOWIE ● 1967
SPACE ODDITY ●
THE MAN WHO SOLD THE WORLD ● 70
HUNKY DORY ●
ZIGGY STARDUST ●
ALADDIN SANE ● PIN UPS ●
DIAMOND DOGS ●
YOUNG AMERICANS ●
STATION TO STATION ●
LOW ● HEROES ●
LODGER ●
SCARY MONSTERS ● 80
LET'S DANCE ●
TONIGHT ●
NEVER LET ME DOWN ●
TIN MACHINE ●
90
TIN MACHINE II ●
BLACK TIE WHITE NOISE ●
OUTSIDE ●
EARTHLING ●
'HOURS...' ●
2000
HEATHEN ●
REALITY ●
10
THE NEXT DAY ●
BLACKSTAR ● 16

Genres

Baroque pop
Music hall
Folk rock
Progressive rock
Psychedelic rock
Hard rock
Glam rock
Art rock
Protopunk
Blue-eyed soul
Philly soul
Funk
Krautrock
Electronic
Ambient
World
New wave
Post-punk
Dance
Post-disco
Pop
Soul
Industrial rock
Alternative rock
Drum and bass
Jungle
Techno
Avant-garde jazz

Sources: Wikipedia; IMDb; *Rolling Stone*; *NME*; *The Economist*

Why eating chocolate is good for you

For lots of people there is little doubt about the deliciousness of chocolate. But its health benefits are less clear. Chocolate has been implicated in causing a litany of problems, including acne and obesity. In large enough quantities it even has the potential to poison people. But in recent years studies have found that eating small amounts of the right kind of chocolate can actually be healthy. Why? The short answer lies in the chemistry of chocolate.

First, cocoa beans are packed with flavonoids, which are natural antioxidants. One in particular, called epicatechin, seems especially effective in helping the body get rid of free-radicals, which may help preserve cell membranes and ward off cardiovascular disease. But flavonoids degrade quickly when heated or processed and are often removed from commercial chocolate because they taste bitter. So only raw cocoa and, to a lesser extent, dark chocolate, offer these benefits.

Second, cocoa contains a stimulant called theobromine, which has some positive health effects. Theobromine has a very similar molecular structure to caffeine. But while caffeine's effects are more prominent in the central nervous system, one of theobromine's well-known effects is on the heart. By increasing the heartbeat and dilating blood vessels, it can reduce blood pressure. It may also boost "good" rather than "bad" cholesterol and stop plaque building up on artery walls. Theobromine can even help alleviate symptoms of asthma because it helps relax the body's smooth muscle, such as that found in the lungs. Some studies suggest it is better at suppressing coughs than codeine. Last and perhaps most surprising of all, chocolate may fight tooth decay more effectively than fluoride. Theobromine appears to help with repairing enamel and protecting teeth from further erosion by acids.

For all these benefits, there is a dark side to chocolate. In rare cases, eating too much chocolate can lead to theobromine poisoning, which can be lethal – but more often causes nausea, trembling or headaches. The danger is even more acute for animals.

Small dogs, for example, can die from eating as little as 100g of milk chocolate. This is because their bodies cannot metabolise theobromine quickly enough. In 2014, four bears were found dead in New Hampshire after demolishing 90lb of chocolate and junk food; all four died of heart attacks. Even so, for most people the occasional piece of chocolate remains a safe and even healthy pleasure.

Shape shifter: Batman on film – how has his physique changed?

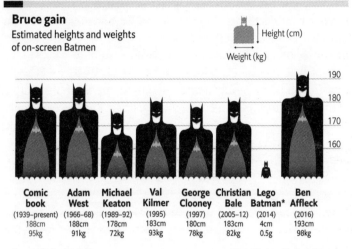

Bruce gain
Estimated heights and weights
of on-screen Batmen

Height (cm)

Weight (kg)

Comic book	**Adam West**	**Michael Keaton**	**Val Kilmer**	**George Clooney**	**Christian Bale**	**Lego Batman***	**Ben Affleck**
(1939–present)	(1966–68)	(1989–92)	(1995)	(1997)	(2005–12)	(2014)	(2016)
188cm	188cm	178cm	183cm	180cm	183cm	4cm	193cm
95kg	91kg	72kg	93kg	78kg	82kg	0.5g	98kg

190
180
170
160

Sources: Moviepilot; IMDb

*From *The Lego Movie*, not to scale

Bruce Wayne appears to have installed a weight-bench in the Batcave. In a promotional poster for *Batman v Superman: Dawn of Justice*, you might be surprised by the imposing brawn of Ben Affleck (the latest to interpret the role of orphan-billionaire-turned-nocturnal-vigilante), who sends a steely glare across to Henry Cavill's Superman. Superman has always been bulky – but in their first Hollywood appearance together, Batman looks the physically superior of the two. A recent red-carpet interview with Affleck revealed why: "This isn't the Adam West days. You can't just roll out of bed and put the suit on. Audiences expect you to look like a superhero."

Ironically, data collected by Moviepilot suggest that since Batman first appeared in feature-length films 50 years ago, West has been the closest in physique to the Gotham crusader as specified in the comic books: 6' 2" (1.88m) tall, and weighing 210lb (95kg). Yet few would name West's portrayal as the best. It is hard not to scoff at his unflattering spandex getup (the moulded Batsuits were only introduced with Michael Keaton's 1989 version) and his unrealistic scrapes with death. By contrast, the muscled-up Batman of the Christopher Nolan trilogy – played by Christian Bale – was lauded by critics, despite being a little undersized.

Not meeting the exact physical blueprint of Wayne is not a catastrophe in modern cinema. Keaton was the most diminutive of the actors to play Batman, weighing just 159lb and reaching only 5' 10". To compensate, the slight superhero was shot in narrow doorways (giving the illusion of breadth) or near to the camera, and other characters constantly referred to a "six-foot bat". George Clooney was also a little short for the role, but appeared bulky and imposing in the ill-fated *Batman and Robin* (1997). He never shared screen-time with the "super soldier" Bane, and only fought the hilarious Mr Freeze (Arnold Schwarzenegger) hand-to-hand at the film's climax.

Later Batmen did not require such choreography. Val Kilmer's sturdy build spoke for itself, with some help from the script: Nicole Kidman, his love interest, lasciviously implored us to gaze at his "eyes, [his] lips, [his] body". Bale trained topless in *Batman Begins* (2005) and *The Dark Knight Rises* (2012). Not to be outdone, Affleck stars in a semi-nude and perspiration-filled training montage featuring tyres and chains.

The villains have also become more physically imposing. Where West tussled with explosive sharks, Clooney contended with a frozen Gotham, and Heath Ledger's Oscar-winning anarchic Joker "want[ed] to watch the world burn", recent enemies have been henchman-like. Tom Hardy's Bane, in the final Nolan film, achieves his malicious goals by crushing windpipes and smashing skulls. For once, we saw the caped crusader outmuscled, as his opponent lifted him into the air and crashed him to the floor, wondering aloud: "What would break first... [his] spirit, or [his] body?"

To conquer his latest nemesis – a superhuman from the planet Krypton – Wayne has piled on even more pounds. Yet the role of

Batman demands stealth as much as strength. Affleck is certainly physically impressive and achieves his goal of looking "like a superhero", but lumbers around like a human bull in a Gotham china shop. In the past 50 years, Batman has foiled evil plots by using his brain as much as, if not more than, his brawn. His battles have been less physical, more psychological. Perhaps it is time to put the weight-bench away. When it comes to Batman, bigger isn't always better.

Why Indians love cricket so much

To outsiders, the magnitude of Indians' love for cricket is as incomprehensible as its feverish intensity. In February 2014, India awarded the Bharat Ratna, its highest civilian honour, to Sachin Tendulkar, a recently retired batsman. Millions in India, a country of 1.3 billion people and only one nationally popular game, celebrated wildly. When India's national side plays a big game, an estimated 400 million watch on television. Yet cricket's take-off in India is a highly improbable development. The game is difficult to play properly, requiring space, a good turf pitch and expensive equipment – which only a small handful of Indian cricketers have access to. Most will never strap on pads or bowl with a leather ball. So why do Indians so love the game?

Contrary to what many believe, India's success at cricket does not explain it; if it did, hockey would be far more popular. Between 1928 and 1956, India's hockey team won six consecutive Olympic gold medals, a domination Indian cricketers have never threatened to rival. Despite having more cricketers than the rest of the world put together, India has only fairly recently become consistently competitive at cricket.

Nor was cricket's conquest of India a colonial ruse. India's 19th-century British rulers never intended to proselytise their favourite game. But this proved to be the original, and perhaps most important, reason for its astonishing spread. Anxious for the prestige that the British attached to the game, some of the richest and most ambitious Indians – including Parsi and Hindu business communities in Bombay and princely rulers elsewhere – began playing it off their own bat (as it were). Thus, cricket became a game of the Indian elite, loaded with political significance which it has never lost. The fact that Jawaharlal Nehru, India's first prime minister, also opened the batting for the Indian Parliament side was a symbol of a wider retention of British culture and institutions. No other sport has ever received such top-level patronage in India.

But Indian cricket was not only elite. From its earliest days in

Bombay, it was also popular. Vast crowds turned out to watch the first Parsi and Hindu teams take on their colonial rulers, and each other. This reflected the time and place; surging growth in Bombay's textile factories had spawned a new class of organised labour, with a modicum of spare time and money. It perhaps also reflected the hierarchic nature of traditional Indian society.

More recently, the game's popularity has been massively increased with the growth of mass media – especially television. In 1989, India had around 30 million households with a television. Now it has over 160 million, an explosion that has been partly driven by cricket, because it is what Indians most want to watch. In turn, India's cricket fan-base has been many times multiplied, and the character of the national game has changed. No longer elite, Indian cricket is now emphatically populist. What was once an English summer game has become in India a celebrity-infused, highly politicised, billion-dollar industry. In this confection, cricket's storied gentlemanly ideals, of good manners and fair play, are at best only dimly apparent.

Geek speak: technically speaking

How to trace a cyber-weapon

The internet has changed all sorts of industries, from book delivery to newspaper publishing to pornography. Spying is no exception. In November 2014, Symantec, a US anti-virus firm, announced the discovery of Regin, a complicated piece of malicious software that has been lurking on computer networks in Russia and Saudi Arabia (among other places), stealing whatever secrets have come its way. Only a couple of weeks before, Kaspersky Labs, another anti-virus firm, revealed the existence of DarkHotel, another piece of espionage-ware that targeted corporate bosses and other bigwigs staying at hotels in Asia. Both pieces of software were slick, sophisticated and complicated. For that reason, the anti-virus firms think they were the work of nation states. DarkHotel was tentatively pinned on South Korea. Regin is thought to have been the work of the British, possibly with help from the Americans. But how do anti-virus researchers know where viruses come from?

The answer is that they don't, at least not for certain. Indeed, one of the attractions of computerised spying (for the spooks at least) is that it is much more difficult to figure out who is behind any given campaign. Unlike human spies, computer code does not speak with an accent; nor does it have a cover story that can be investigated. So anti-virus researchers must rely on inference, guesswork and any small clues they can scrape together. One of the most famous bits of nation-state malware, Stuxnet, was used to sabotage centrifuges used by Iran's nuclear programme. Suspicion naturally fell on Israel, which is the region's most technologically advanced nation, and which has long feared that Iran is working on a nuclear bomb (there have been rumours that Israel has considered air strikes against Iranian factories). The US, as Israel's chief ally and one of Iran's chief opponents, fell under suspicion as well. Neither country has ever admitted to working on Stuxnet. But American officials have never denied it, either.

Sometimes the code itself can contain clues. DarkHotel's targets, for instance, were mostly in Asia (the largest number of targets were from India, Japan and China). The computer code contained Korean characters, as well as the online alias of a South Korean programmer. One of Regin's modules is called "LEGSPIN", a cricketing term, which might narrow the field of suspects. And the researchers who analysed it have pointed out that Regin seems to be very similar (or perhaps even identical) to the software used in an attack on Belgacom, a big Belgian telecommunications firm whose clients include the main institutions of the EU. Leaks from Edward Snowden, a former US spy, have linked that attack to the British.

But all this is tentative. The spies presumably know that their opponents (as well as civilian security researchers) will try to reverse-engineer any computerised bugs they stumble across. So either the clues that do remain were included accidentally, or they are deliberately designed to deceive. Mikko Hypponen, the boss of F-secure, a Finnish anti-virus firm, points out that early Russian attempts at computerised espionage were deliberately designed to look like they came from China. As always with cases of spying and espionage, nothing is ever certain.

How online advertisers read your mind

Anyone who has ever used the internet will be familiar with the feeling of déjà vu. You land on a website you might never have been to before, only to see advertisements that show something familiar: a pair of shoes you have shopped for, for example, or a hotel you looked up but did not book. Are advertisers psychic, or snooping?

Technology means advertisements can be targeted more accurately than ever before. As people spend more time online, they share more of their data with websites, e-mail services and social networks. Google has a big business delivering advertisements related to the topics people search for, and facilitating targeted ads on websites owned by others. Social networks like Facebook and Twitter track people's movements around the web and enable advertisers to reach users via tailored advertisements. Thousands of other firms track where people shop, what they buy online and infer other information about them, such as their job and income. One way they do this is through "cookies", tiny snippets of data stored in users' web browsers that allow websites to identify those users (not by name, but by a unique ID). Firms can then track what sort of articles people read, where they shop, their location and other details, and can build up profiles of consumers.

This allows advertisers to reach people they think are most likely to be interested in hearing from them – which explains web users' frequent sense of déjà vu. For example, advertisers can decide to show ads only to people who have shopped on a particular website before but left before clicking "buy". In industry parlance, this is called "retargeting". Advertisers know the cookie IDs of users who have come to their website, or can buy that information from another firm, and then advertise only to those users. Increasingly this is done via an automated auction process, called "real-time bidding". The website where an advertising slot needs filling sends information about the user and the page where the ad would run to an online advertising exchange, where advertisers decide whether they want to bid on that particular slot, usually offering more if it is a user who has shown interest in their product in the past. The entire process happens in a fraction of a second; and that is how ads appear to read your mind, and follow you around the web.

Clever (and spooky) though that is, online advertising technology is becoming even more sophisticated. In addition to being able to reach particular users, advertisers can modify their ads to make them even more relevant. For example, if a user has browsed a carmaker's website and looked at a particular model, the advertiser might put a picture of that type of car in the ad. In the winter, a fashion retailer might show images of heavy coats to users in New York, but sandals to people browsing in Hawaii. Advertisers now have more control, too, about the time of day their ads appear and which sort of devices they want to send ads to. They can infer income, for example, from what sort of device or operating system a consumer has: people with Apple computers tend to be richer than those with PCs. Advertising is not exactly a science yet, but it is becoming more of one.

The best time to post a selfie (or anything else) on Facebook

Probability of getting a like, comment or share in response to a facebook post
By city of residence*, October 15th 2014 to February 11th 2015

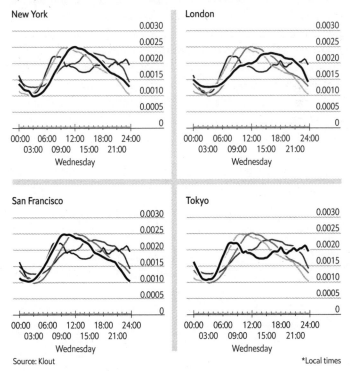

New York

London

San Francisco

Tokyo

Source: Klout

*Local times

When is the best time to post something on Facebook? If you're looking for a response, then don't go for a lazy Sunday. A study from Klout, a social-media analytics website based in San Francisco, suggests that the working week is a better bet. The answer also varies by location. New Yorkers might live in the city that never sleeps, but the data show that they lag behind San Franciscans in their peak reaction times to Facebook posts. Londoners tend to engage with Facebook later in the day, as work is winding down. Tokyo residents are best at separating work and play – they are most likely to respond outside normal working hours. This gives social networkers a good indication of when best to post, and also where the most Facebook-friendly offices tend to be. News organisations, which are increasingly dependent on Facebook's 1.6 billion users for traffic, can also take note.

Why video-games are expensive to make

When Activision, a big games publisher, released *Destiny* in September 2014, it was not just covered in the gaming press. Many newspapers commented on the game's eye-watering budget, reported to be around $500 million. How could a video game cost half a billion dollars to make? The truth is, it didn't – Activision wanted *Destiny* to be the first game in a long-running franchise, and was prepared to spend $500 million to make that happen. But game budgets are, nonetheless, swelling. Developers and publishers are coy about releasing specific numbers, but budgets of tens of millions of dollars are not uncommon. The biggest, most polished games can cost hundreds of millions. *Star Wars: The Old Republic*, an online game released in 2011, is reputed to have cost between $150 million and $200 million. *Grand Theft Auto V*, which came out two years later, reputedly cost $265 million. These are numbers on the same scale as blockbuster Hollywood films. Why have games become so expensive to make?

One reason is Moore's law. Computer graphics have improved enormously in the past 20 years; the graphics in *Destiny*, which was created by a team of around 500 people, are streets ahead of those in *Doom*, a seminal shooter released in 1993 that was written by a handful of friends. With a few exceptions (such as *SpeedTree*, a piece of software that automates the creation of realistic-looking trees), all the art in a video game is hand-crafted. As characters, items, levels and visual effects have become more intricate and detailed, developers have had little choice but to throw more and more artists at the problem. Another reason costs are rising is the increasing professionalism of the industry. These days, Hollywood actors are hired (and paid handsomely) to voice characters. The biggest developers market-test their products to destruction. Like political parties honing a slogan, they offer snippets of gameplay to focus groups. If anything is found to be too difficult, too obscure or simply not fun, it is sent back to be re-done. That kind of quality control costs serious money.

But comparisons with the film industry can be misleading. Movie budgets typically include only the cost of actually making the film. Game budgets often include marketing costs, too. As games have become a mainstream pastime, those have become enormous. A blockbuster game such as *Battlefield 3*, released in 2011, will be advertised in newspapers, on television, on billboards and online. Publishers throw glitzy launch parties featuring stunts like driving a tank down London's Oxford Street. All that can cost more than paying the coders and artists who produced the game in the first place. That said, when it comes to quantity of entertainment, games are bigger than films. The biggest-budget games tend to be those that deposit their players into giant, open-ended worlds and invite them to explore. Whereas film sets are seen only from a few carefully chosen shots, game worlds must survive inspection from every angle, by millions of players who can roam around at will. And while few films run much beyond three hours, even a short game will offer ten or more hours of play; many offer several times that.

Rising game budgets have created breathtaking, cinematic experiences. But not everyone is happy. Higher costs have made publishers timid, preferring to serve up more of what their customers like rather than risk tens of millions of dollars on something new and untried. Lists of bestselling games have come to resemble Hollywood blockbuster charts: full of sequels, reboots and minor variations on old, reliable formulas. Dissatisfied developers have left to strike out on their own, recreating the garage atmosphere of game development 20 or 30 years ago. With smaller budgets, and less design by committee, indie games companies are where much of the industry's innovation is taking place. Many make a virtue of their lo-fi graphics (the blocky visuals of Minecraft being the most famous example). Mobile games, played in short bursts on tiny screens with limited interfaces, don't need big budgets either. But it is still the big-budget games that rake in the cash. *Grand Theft Auto V* earned around $800 million on its first day – three times what it cost to make. And with the latest games consoles capable of rendering even more detailed graphics, expect budgets to keep climbing.

How virtual reality works

If Facebook, Sony and HTC have their way, the most coveted consumer technology product of 2016 will not be a smartphone or a giant, paper-thin flatscreen TV. It will be a virtual-reality (VR) headset: computerised goggles that transport users to an immersive, three-dimensional universe. Here they can watch panoramic films, take virtual tours or experience whatever other alluring distractions a growing group of VR programmers might dream up. How does the technology behind the vision work?

Brendan Iribe, the co-founder of Oculus, a VR startup that was bought for $2 billion by Facebook in 2014, describes VR as a "hack on the human sensory system". It makes sense, then, for VR companies to focus their hacking efforts on the sense that humans rely on most: vision. Humans have stereoscopic vision, which means that they perceive depth by noting the subtle differences between the images received by each of their eyes. VR headsets have two tiny screens, one for each eye, which exploit that. By carefully altering the images fed to each eye, the user's brain is persuaded that it is looking at an entire three-dimensional world instead of a pair of flat images.

The next trick is to make it seem as if that world surrounds the user. Modern VR headsets are fitted with tiny sensors similar to those used in smartphones – accelerometers, gyroscopes and the like – which can keep track of the movements of the wearer's head. When the user looks around, the computer can then update the view on the screens. But those sensors must update themselves dozens of times a second, and errors accumulate quickly. So headsets may also be equipped with LEDs. That allows a camera, mounted elsewhere in the room, to keep track of the headset and to correct errors in the embedded sensors as they accumulate. It also allows the computer to keep track of the user's body. That allows hand-held controls to give users a pair of virtual arms and hands, and means that walking forward in the real world results in movement in the virtual one.

That all sounds fairly simple in theory. But building a usable headset stretches modern computing technology to its limits (during the last wave of VR hype, in the 1990s, it became clear that technology was not up to the task). For VR to work, the illusion must be extraordinarily slick. Humans are extremely sensitive to visual inconsistencies; even small snags can cause "VR sickness", an affliction like motion-sickness. So images must update very quickly. That requires beefy computing hardware capable of generating 90 or more frames of animation a second. And the sensors that track the user's head must be able to talk to the computer at least that fast: any delay can cause an unpleasant dragging sensation. Despite the difficulties, engineers are convinced that such problems have, at last, been banished. The question now is how many people will be prepared to pay for a fancy VR headset – particularly when smartphones slotted into a much cheaper adaptor can offer a comparable experience at a tiny fraction of the price.

How machine learning works

The standard joke about artificial intelligence (AI) is that, like nuclear fusion, it has been the future for more than half a century now. In 1958 the *New York Times* reported that the Perceptron, an early AI machine developed at Cornell University with military money, was "the embryo of an electronic computer that [the American Navy] expects will be able to walk, talk, see, write, reproduce itself and be conscious of its existence". Five decades later, self-aware battleships remain conspicuous by their absence. Yet alongside the hype, there has been spectacular progress: computers are now better than any human at the games of chess and Go, for instance. Computers can process human speech and read even messy handwriting. To many people today, automated telephone-response systems are infuriating. But they would seem like magic to someone from the 1950s. These days AI is in the news again, for there has been impressive progress in the past few years in a particular subfield of AI called machine learning. But what exactly is it?

Machine learning is exactly what it sounds like: an attempt to perform a trick that even very primitive animals are capable of, namely learning from experience. Computers are hyper-literal, ornery beasts: anyone who has tried programming one will tell you that the difficulty comes from dealing with the fact that a computer will do exactly and precisely what you tell it to, stupid mistakes and all. For tasks that can be boiled down into simple, unambiguous rules – such as crunching through difficult mathematics, for instance – that is fine. For woollier jobs, it is a serious problem, especially because humans themselves might struggle to articulate clear rules. In 1964 Potter Stewart, a US Supreme Court judge, found it impossibly difficult to set a legally watertight definition of pornography. Frustrated, he famously wrote that, although he could not define porn as such, "I know it when I see it." Machine learning aims to help computers discover such fuzzy rules by themselves, without having to be explicitly instructed every step of the way by human programmers.

There are many different kinds of machine learning. But the one that is grabbing headlines at the moment is called "deep learning". It uses artificial neural networks – simplified computer simulations of how biological neurons behave – to extract rules and patterns from sets of data. Show a neural network enough pictures of cats, for instance, or have it listen to enough German speech, and it will be able to tell you if a picture it has never seen before is a cat, or a sound recording is in German. The general approach is not new (the Perceptron, mentioned above, was one of the first neural networks). But the ever-increasing power of computers has allowed deep-learning machines to simulate billions of neurons. At the same time, the huge quantity of information available on the internet has provided the algorithms with an unprecedented quantity of data to chew on. The results can be impressive. Facebook's Deep Face algorithm, for instance, is about as good as a human being when it comes to recognising specific faces, even if they are poorly lit, or seen from a strange angle. E-mail spam is much less of a problem than it used to be, because the vast quantities of it circulating online have allowed computers to learn to recognise what a spam e-mail looks like, and divert it before it ever reaches your inbox.

Big firms like Google, Baidu and Microsoft are pouring resources into AI development, aiming to improve search results, build computers you can talk to, and more. A wave of startups wants to use the techniques for everything from looking for tumours in medical images to automating back-office work like the preparation of sales reports. The appeal of automated voice or facial-recognition for spies and policemen is obvious, and they are also taking a keen interest. This rapid progress has spawned prophets of doom, who worry that computers could become cleverer than their human masters and perhaps even displace them. Such worries are not entirely without foundation. Even now, scientists do not really understand how the brain works. But there is nothing supernatural about it – and that implies that building something similar inside a machine should be possible in principle. Some conceptual breakthrough, or the steady rise in computing power, might one day give rise to hyper-intelligent, self-aware computers. But for now, and for the foreseeable future, deep-learning machines will remain pattern-recognition engines. They are not going to take over the world. But they will shake up the world of work.

Tech-tonic shifts

San Francisco, Silicon Valley and the strip of land that runs along the shore of the Bay between them have had a tremendous decade as the hub of the global technology industry. The area's biggest companies have soared to heights once unimaginable, coming to represent all that the world finds most exciting about US capitalism. The Valley has revolutionised nearly every aspect of the global economy, transforming how firms make decisions, people make friends and protesters make a fuss.

Today's tech firms touch more people more quickly than ever before, partly due to the global increase in smartphone use. As a result, they are growing faster and attracting more money. The figures are eye-watering: Uber, a ride-hailing company, is valued at $41 billion; Airbnb, a firm through which people turn their homes or spare rooms into hotels, is valued at $26 billion. Such success makes it easier to attract wealthy venture capitalists, allowing today's startups to stay private for longer (and avoid regulatory risks). It used to be extremely rare to find a startup valued over $1 billion, but by mid-2015 there were 74 of these so-called "unicorns" in America's tech sector, valued at $273 billion in total.

As the fortunes of startups have moved upwards, so too have their physical locations. In the 1990s most of the activity was to the south, in areas like Palo Alto and Mountain View, which is still where the area's big public companies are mostly based. But today younger private firms prefer to be much closer to the city itself: Uber, Dropbox, Pinterest and Airbnb all have their headquarters in San Francisco.

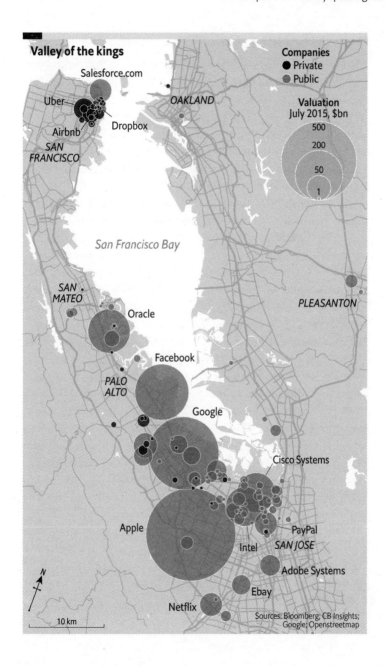

Valley of the kings

Salesforce.com

Uber

Airbnb

Dropbox

SAN FRANCISCO

OAKLAND

Companies
- Private
- Public

Valuation
July 2015, $bn
500
200
50
1

San Francisco Bay

SAN MATEO

Oracle

PLEASANTON

Facebook

PALO ALTO

Google

Cisco Systems

Apple

PayPal

Intel

SAN JOSE

Adobe Systems

Ebay

Netflix

N

10 km

Sources: Bloomberg; CB Insights;
Google; Openstreetmap

How technology made fashion week passé

Fashion designers should love fashion week. It is the culmination of months of work. Celebrities clamour to attend their shows, then study each model as if the world's future rested on the cut of a skirt. But designers are pouting about the six-monthly ritual – so much so that the Council of Fashion Designers of America (CFDA) commissioned America's perhaps least glamorous group, management consultants, to explore their complaints. The Boston Consulting Group interviewed more than 50 people, including designers, editors, bloggers and retailers. So why, did its report conclude, is fashion week no longer fashionable?

Fashion week used to serve a distinct purpose. Designers would prepare collections and present clothes to the press, to major retailers and to other industry insiders. Fashion editors would then prepare sumptuous magazine spreads featuring the clothes they liked best. Retailers would order this or that dress. About four to six months later, those clothes would appear in shops.

Technology has upended all this. As soon as models sashay down the runway, photographs are posted online and shared endlessly across social media. Fast-fashion brands copy (though the industry prefers the euphemism "interpret") designers' styles, often stocking look-alikes in their shops before designers' own clothes make it to department stores. When designers' clothes finally arrive, they seem stale. It is no coincidence that the industry's top two retailers are TJX (the company behind TJ Maxx/TK Maxx) and Inditex. TJX buys brand-name clothes from stores that can't sell them at full price, and offers them at a deep discount. Inditex owns Zara, the pioneer in fast fashion.

Few designers like the current system. Less obvious is what they should replace it with. One idea is for fashion houses to show clothes only to certain people, such as retailers and some press, behind closed doors. Designers would then stage a bigger, public presentation a few months later, when those clothes are available in stores. There would, of course, be the threat that some images would leak. Another idea would be to continue the current system, but make a small subset of clothes available immediately. Designers are already testing new ideas. Burberry and Tom Ford, for example, have said that their September 2016 fashion shows would showcase clothes available immediately. For the foreseeable future, experimentation will be in vogue.

What is code?

From lifts to cars to airliners to smartphones, modern civilisation is powered by software, the digital instructions that allow computers, and the devices they control, to perform calculations and respond to their surroundings. How did that software get there? Someone had to write it. But code, the sequences of symbols painstakingly created by programmers, is not quite the same as software, the sequences of instructions that computers execute. So what exactly is it?

Coding, or programming, is a way of writing instructions for computers that bridges the gap between how humans like to express themselves and how computers actually work. Programming languages, of which there are hundreds, cannot generally be executed by computers directly. Instead, programs written in a particular "high level" language such as C++, Python or Java are translated by a special piece of software (a compiler or an interpreter) into low-level instructions which a computer can actually run. In some cases programmers write software in low-level instructions directly, but this is fiddly. It is usually much easier to use a high-level programming language, because such languages make it easier to express complex, abstract ideas or commands efficiently and accurately; they also absolve programmers from having to worry about tedious details relating to the innards of the particular computer on which the program will eventually run. A program written in a high-level language can therefore be made to run on all sorts of different computers.

Programming languages exist in many families and styles, rather like human languages. There are many dialects of C, for example; there are families of "functional" programming languages; and there are languages optimised for "parallel processing" (where several programs run alongside each other to accomplish a particular task, such as image processing or weather forecasting). As with human languages, these programming languages are all capable of expressing the same ideas, and in theory any program can be written in any language. But in practice some languages are better suited to some uses than others, just as French is traditionally used for diplomacy and English is the international language of business. And just as knowing a few different spoken languages makes it easier to learn another one, the same is true of programming languages. Once you understand common features (loops, recursion, conditionals, regular expressions and so on) you can usually pick up a new language quickly, particularly if it's reasonably close to another language you already know.

Writing a program and then running it is magic, in a way. The numbers, letters and symbols of code are transmuted into instructions executed by microscopic circuits to achieve the desired results. Pixels appear on the screen; lifts move; airline tickets are ordered; lists are sorted; e-mails are delivered. But just because the results seem magical does not mean that coding is mysterious and inaccessible. Indeed, one of the joys of coding is that computers are the opposite of mysterious: they operate in an unforgivingly predictable, consistent and deterministic manner. Most people do not need to be able to write code to do their jobs, any more than they need to be able to speak foreign languages or do algebra. But it is useful to have some basic experience in coding, and not just to demystify how computers work. As Marc Andreessen, the co-creator of the Netscape web browser, likes to say, in future there will be two kinds of jobs: those that involve telling computers what to do, and those that involve being told what to do by computers. If you're worried that your job is in danger of being automated away by software, then learning to code could be a useful insurance policy. Even if you're not, coding can also be fun.

Never gonna put you down

Smartphone use
% reporting use by hour of the day, over a week*

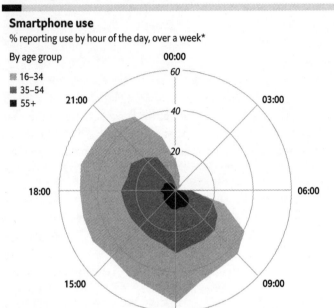

By age group
- 16–34
- 35–54
- 55+

Source: Ofcom   *1,644 British adults surveyed between February and April 2014

Earth is rapidly becoming a planet of the phones. Today more than two billion smartphones are in use worldwide, and that is expected to double by the end of the decade. By then, nearly 80% of adults will have a device in their pocket with processing power that would have passed for a supercomputer not many years ago. To get an idea of how much time people will then spend on their smartphones it helps to look at today's young people: the chart shows that they report much more use at all times of the day than older generations. In total, according to Ofcom, Britain's telecoms regulator, those aged between 16 and 24 use their devices for nearly four hours a day; those between 55 and 64 only half as much. When assessing overall screen time, however, the smartphone still has some catching up to do to match longer-established technologies like television.

The trouble with space junk

According to NASA, America's space agency, the skies high above the Earth are cluttered up with around 23,000 pieces of man-made space junk measuring 10cm or more across, zipping along at great speed and posing a threat to working satellites. The European Space Agency reckons that collision alerts arising from worn-out satellites, defunct rockets and other clutter (such as launch adapters, lens covers, copper wires and the odd glove) have doubled in the past decade. Every such collision spawns more junk – a phenomenon known as the Kessler syndrome, named after Donald Kessler, an American physicist who postulated it in the 1970s. Why is space junk such a growing problem?

Low-Earth orbit, the region between 160 and 2,000km above the Earth, is crucial to space exploration. It is home to about half of the roughly 1,300 satellites which scan the Earth in great detail for both military and civilian purposes. It is also littered with "around 5,000 objects that are either rocket bodies or dead payloads," says Kessler. This is dangerous. A fleck of paint travelling at an orbital velocity of 17,500kph can dent a spacecraft, kill an astronaut or do enough damage to throw a satellite off course. Inoperative rockets are prone to random explosions of the unused fuel they carry. In February 2015, a snag in an American weather satellite's battery caused it to explode. The incident scattered more than 100 new fragments of junk into space. In 2007, China deliberately blasted one of its own spacecraft into smithereens to test an anti-satellite weapon; two years later a Russian satellite accidentally took out an American one. Those incidents alone increased the amount of orbiting space debris by one-third. Future missions will face significant new constraints if such littering continues unchecked.

Space agencies and private companies from various countries have proposed a variety of methods to clean up the mess. Scientists in Japan have recommended installing lasers on the International Space Station to nudge debris into the Earth's atmosphere, where it would burn up harmlessly. NASA scientists have proposed doing the same thing using ground-based lasers. In March 2015, the European Space Agency experimented with nets designed to capture moving debris. Japan Aerospace Exploration Agency has devised an electrodynamic tether which, when tied to a piece of space junk, would cause it to slow down and fall into a lower orbit. Space agencies across the globe are considering other options too. Dead satellites located in geosynchronous orbit (about 36,000km above the surface of the Earth) are sometimes pushed into a "graveyard orbit" about 300km further out. New technologies allow rockets that have delivered their payloads to reignite their engines, lower their orbits and then burn up in the Earth's atmosphere. Many countries have agreed that satellites should be designed to burn up harmlessly in the atmosphere within 25 years of their operational lifespan coming to an end.

There is no shortage of ideas, in short. But fixing the problem is still difficult. "There is no international regulatory agency to enforce [these rules]," says Kessler. Space agencies and commercial satellite operators are reluctant to dedicate precious fuel, or reduce the working lifetime of a satellite, to ensure that celestial last rites are performed properly. Fiddling with junk belonging to other countries is problematic, too. "Under the current international legal system, the launching state has perpetual sovereign rights and control over objects they put into orbit," says Brian Weeden, an expert on space debris at Secure World Foundation, a think-tank. Of the 22,000 catalogued pieces of orbital junk known in 2012, only 16,000 have a known launching state. Even when ownership is known, it is not clear who would be responsible if such bodies were accidentally nudged in the wrong direction, only to blow up prematurely. Working within these constraints, the US Department of Defense (and startups, which charge a fee) share information about debris trajectories to help other agencies avoid trouble. The problem is tricky, but not insoluble; Kessler estimates that removing the 500 most dangerous objects, even at the slow rate of five a year, would solve most of the problem at a modest cost. The technology exists to do it; the obstacles are chiefly regulatory.

How Bitcoin works

Bitcoin, the world's "first decentralised digital currency", was launched in 2009 by a mysterious person known only by the pseudonym Satoshi Nakamoto, whose true identity is still unknown. Since then, the value of a single Bitcoin has fluctuated wildly, reaching a high of around $1,000 in late 2013 before falling to less than half that level, and then rebounding in 2016. What exactly is Bitcoin, and how does it work?

Unlike traditional currencies, which are issued by central banks, Bitcoin has no central monetary authority. Instead it is underpinned by a peer-to-peer computer network made up of its users' machines, akin to the networks that underpin BitTorrent, a file-sharing system, and Skype, an audio, video and chat service. Bitcoins are mathematically generated as the computers in this network execute difficult number-crunching tasks, a procedure known as Bitcoin "mining". The mathematics of the Bitcoin system were set up so that it becomes progressively more difficult to "mine" Bitcoins over time, and the total number that can ever be mined is limited to around 21 million. There is therefore no way for a central bank to issue a flood of new Bitcoins and devalue those already in circulation.

The entire network is used to monitor and verify both the creation of new Bitcoins through mining, and the transfer of Bitcoins between users. A log is collectively maintained of all transactions, with every new transaction broadcast across the Bitcoin network. Participating machines communicate to create and agree on updates to the official log. This process, which is computationally intensive, is in fact the process used to mine Bitcoins: roughly every 10 minutes, a user whose updates to the log have been approved by the network is awarded a fixed number of new Bitcoins. This has prompted Bitcoin fans to build ever more powerful computers for use in Bitcoin mining.

Bitcoins (or fractions of Bitcoins known as satoshis) can be bought and sold in return for traditional currency on several exchanges, and can also be directly transferred across the internet from one user to another using appropriate software. This makes Bitcoin a potentially attractive currency in which to settle international transactions, without messing around with bank charges or exchange rates. Some internet services (such as web hosting and online gambling) can be paid for using Bitcoin. The complexity and opacity of the system means it also appeals to those with more nefarious purposes in mind, such as money laundering or paying for illegal drugs. But most people will be reluctant to adopt Bitcoin while the software required to use it remains so complex, and the value of an individual Bitcoin is so volatile. Just as BitTorrent was not the first file-sharing service and Skype was not the first voice-over-internet service, it may be that Bitcoin will be a pioneer in the field of virtual currencies, but will be overshadowed by an easier-to-use rival.

The life scientific

How to search for time travellers

As well as being a staple of science fiction, time travel is also the inspiration for serious (or at least semi-serious) speculation by theorists. Some have devoted themselves to working out how it might be possible in theory, if difficult in practice, to build a time machine using exotic configurations of black holes, wormholes or cosmic strings. Others have considered whether a "self-consistency principle" operates to ensure that time travellers cannot cause paradoxical situations by, for example, going back in time and murdering their own ancestors. Then there are those who have taken an experimental approach, and searched for time travellers directly. How do they do it?

One idea, tried by Amal Dorai, a graduate student at the Massachusetts Institute of Technology (MIT), is to hold a convention for time travellers and see if any show up. He held such an event in May 2005, invitations for which were slipped into obscure library books or added to time capsules, in the hope that they would be found in the far future when time travel had become possible. Visitors from the future were asked to land their time machines on the MIT volleyball court, which was reserved for the occasion. But of the 450 people who attended the event, none claimed to be time travellers. In 2009, the British physicist Stephen Hawking performed a variation of this experiment, holding a party for time travellers, but sending out the invitations after the event had taken place, so that only visitors from the future could possibly attend. But nobody came. Dr Hawking said this constituted "experimental evidence that time travel is not possible".

The latest twist in this unusual field is to use the internet to search for evidence of time travel, an approach proposed by Robert Nemiroff and Teresa Wilson of Michigan Technological University. They scoured the internet for "prescient" information – in other words, online posts suggesting knowledge of the future. In particular, they looked for two distinctive phrases that emerged at specific times: "Comet Ison" (the name of a comet discovered in

September 2012) and "Pope Francis" (the name taken by Jorge Mario Bergoglio when he became pope in March 2013). Any mention of these terms before the dates in question might be the work of time travellers. But analysis of Google, Facebook and Twitter usage, and examination of the search logs of a popular astronomical website, did not produce any evidence of time travel.

Of course, this does not prove that time travel is impossible. It may be that time travellers are not interested in comets or the pope, or prefer to keep a low profile. Some theorists reckon that if a time machine is ever invented, it will not be possible to travel further back in time than the day of its invention. (If that is the case, the inventor of the first time machine may therefore suddenly be surrounded by time tourists when switching it on.) But this latest experiment is an interesting proof of concept that uses a technology that does exist (the internet) to search for one whose existence is uncertain. The Michigan researchers suggest theirs is "the most sensitive and comprehensive search for time-travellers yet conducted". They are only half joking.

How to debunk a scientific study

Fame, glory and a modest academic salary can all be yours if you write an important scientific study. You might even change the world, as Michael Kremer and Edward Miguel found. They were the authors of an economics paper published in 2004 which showed that giving children deworming tablets increases their school attendance. The study sparked further research into cost-effective interventions in developing countries, all of which has led to millions of children being dewormed every year. Fame can also be won by those who debunk major studies. In July 2015, a team at the London School of Hygiene and Tropical Medicine tried to replicate Kremer and Miguel's study, and found only "some evidence, with high risk of bias" for the original conclusions. Next came the headlines, then the counter-fame, and finally the accusations, back and forth: of researchers capitalising on fame and headlines. Spectators called it the "worm wars". As the dust settled, it seemed that the core message – it is good to deworm children – had not, after all, been debunked. So how does one go about debunking a study properly?

It is crucial to understand the process of discovering an important result. Humans have a useful but unreliable tendency to find patterns amid meaningless noise. Scientists use statistical tests to sniff out sense from the data, but even their tests can sometimes turn up apparent relationships where there are none. To help prevent researchers making a mountain out of a molehill, each of the statistical relationships that scientists publish in their papers comes with a "p-value" attached. This is the probability that their test might have produced the same result if it had been run on random data with no underlying pattern. A lower p-value is better, because this means it less likely the pattern came about for no reason: the usual convention it that a p-value of less than 0.05 is required to consider a finding trustworthy, because that indicates that there is a 95% probability that the result was not merely a random fluke. So one simple way to debunk a paper is to recalculate the results of the original tests (a "strict replication"), hoping to spot an error in the calculation of either the original result or the associated p-value.

Debunkers themselves must beware that they are not committing the opposite sin, of making a molehill out of a mountain. The "power", or sensitivity, of a test is the likelihood that it sniffs out a positive relationship when one is actually there. Higher power is better. One method the medical researchers used in their replication was to cut a large two-year sample of test subjects into two one-year samples. This reduces the sample size, which gives the test less information to go on. This, in turn, reduces the power of the test, meaning that a greater number of positive relationships can sneak by undetected. The original study's authors say this is why the re-analysis was unable to detect the correlation between deworming and school attendance.

So which kind of statistical test should be used for a social-scientific study? Amazingly, there is no one right answer, particularly when multiple disciplines are involved and the data are messy. The medical researchers defended their choice of method as reflecting the common practice in medicine, where tightly controlled and randomised trials are the norm. But methods appropriate to medicine may be too stringent in other contexts, and thus overly dismissive of positive results discovered by economists. Replicators should be forthright about the power of their tests, as much as correlation-hunters must disclose their p-values. The main problem, though, if you wish to debunk a study, is that the underlying data are not usually shared, so replication cannot be done at all. In this instance, the original authors of the worm study had taken the brave and unusual step of making their data widely available. That, ironically, exposed their work to far greater scrutiny than is applied to most studies. Chris Blattman, a professor at Columbia University, urges caution all round: "We should remember that most scientific studies don't stand up to scrutiny very well, and most are utterly wrong." But it is only by trying to replicate or debunk studies that researchers can establish which ones are trustworthy, and which are not.

Why the Zika virus was ignored for so long

On February 1st 2016, the World Health Organisation declared the spread of the Zika virus a global public health emergency. The virus, a suspected cause of birth defects in babies born to mothers who are infected during pregnancy, seems to have come from nowhere. But it has been known about for nearly 70 years. The virus was discovered in 1947, in a rhesus monkey in the Zika forest near the shore of Lake Victoria in Uganda. Researchers studying yellow fever, another virus transmitted by mosquitoes, had put the monkey in a cage hung from a tree, as bait for mosquitoes. Tests of the animal's blood turned up an unknown virus, which also turned up in mosquitoes in the same forest – a clue to how it spread. Why was Zika ignored for so long, and why has it become an emergency now?

Zika was found in a human for the first time in 1952, in Uganda. Nobody knows for sure where or when it began to infect humans. It may have been circulating among monkeys and other animals in the jungle for thousands of years, making the jump to humans relatively recently, carried by mosquitoes. In that regard, Zika is hardly unusual: six in ten infectious diseases in humans have been spread from animals. During the second half of the 20th century, Zika was documented in a handful of people in Africa and Asia. Some studies suggest that it may have been quietly circulating in parts of West Africa and South-East Asia. But it was not of much interest to scientists – and did not alarm public-health hawks – for a long time because it appeared to cause only mild flu-like symptoms, and no massive outbreaks had been reported. Meanwhile, dangerous new pathogens jostled for researchers' and officials' attention: since the 1950s more than 300 contagious diseases have emerged or re-emerged in populations that had never been exposed to them, including HIV/AIDS, SARS, Ebola and antibiotic-resistant bacteria.

Zika may have been infecting many people in Africa for years, staying under the radar of patchy health systems and poor disease surveillance along with any serious health problems that it may have been causing, says Alain Kohl of the University of Glasgow.

Epidemiologists took notice in 2007 when Zika reached Yap, a small Pacific island where, by one estimate, it infected nearly 75% of the population – showing that it could in fact become epidemic. In late 2013, the virus went rampant in French Polynesia, a Pacific archipelago. There, health officials noticed an increase in neurological and auto-immune complications, some causing paralysis.

A surge in these complications, and the birth defects caused by Zika, were easier to spot in Brazil, where the virus arrived in 2015, for two reasons. The first is that many more people were infected with Zika, so spikes in rare complications, such as microcephaly (in which children of infected mothers are born with an abnormally small brain), could be more easily spotted and linked to the virus. The second reason is that the country has a good surveillance system, which was quickly directed to look for cases of Zika and the maladies that it may be causing. That means more cases of the virus, and of the side-effects it can cause, have come to light – and the full extent of the danger it poses has, belatedly, become apparent.

Why cancer has not been cured

Medicine has done a great job of reducing deaths from heart disease and stroke, but less so with cancer. Despite a four-decade war against the disease, costing hundreds of billions of dollars, in the United States alone 1.7 million people are diagnosed with it, and about 600,000 die annually. Why has cancer not been cured?

The main reason is a lack of basic understanding of the molecular mechanisms that drive it. The first medicines to tackle cancer, chemotherapies, were discovered by accident during the second world war, when exposure to nitrogen mustard, a chemical similar to mustard gas, was found to reduce white-blood-cell counts. It and other compounds were then tested to see if they could halt the growth of cancer cells and kill tumours. New drugs were discovered, but little was revealed about the cause of cancer, or why these treatments often worked only temporarily.

Much progress has been made since. Thanks to a deeper understanding of cell biology and genetics, there are now a growing number of targeted therapies designed at a molecular level to recognise particular features specific to cancer cells. Along with chemotherapy, surgery and radiotherapy, these treatments – singly and in combination – have led to a slow but steady increase in survival rates. Childhood cancers and breast cancers are more curable than they used to be. But much work remains to be done. Cancer is seen today less as a disease of specific organs, and more as one of molecular mechanisms caused by the mutation of specific genes. The implication of this shift in thinking is that the best treatment for, say, colorectal cancer may turn out to be a drug designed and approved for use against tumours in an entirely different part of the body.

Another promising new approach, immunotherapy, harnesses the body's own immune system to fight cancer. In trials, it has been successful in inducing long-term remissions of hard-to-treat cancers in about a third of patients. An active area of investigation is predicting which tumours will respond to which therapies. The advent of personalised medicine could herald enormous progress as the fight against cancer continues.

From the depths

A volcanic eruption that started in mid-December 2014 around 65km north-west of Nuku'alofa, the capital of Tonga, and grounded flights to and from the Pacific archipelago for several days, ended a few weeks later, having created the world's youngest land mass: a new island less than 2km across and rising 100 metres above the water's surface. Locals who visited the island in January 2015 said birds had started nesting on it.

Volcanic islands can be valuable. Scientists use Surtsey, which appeared off the coast of Iceland (itself a volcanic island) in 1963, to study the colonisation of virgin land by plants and animals. Since the appearance of Surtsey, at least ten underwater volcanoes have spewed forth enough material to breach the ocean's surface and create new islands. Most are small and erode away soon afterwards. New creations that turn out to have staying power can expand a country's offshore territorial rights. Under the UN Convention on the Law of the Sea, countries can claim rights over fishing, shipping and mining up to 200 nautical miles (370km) from their coasts. A country that claims a new island off its coast can use it as the basis to extend its offshore territorial claims, too.

Niijima, a volcanic island that appeared about 1,000km south of Tokyo in 2013, was at first expected to erode and vanish in short order. But it continued to grow, and in 2014 it merged with an older volcanic island, Nishinoshima. The joint land mass is still increasing in size. Once it settles down, and if it looks likely to survive, Japan may make a new claim. Coastal erosion and rising sea levels mean that the sea often takes away land. But every now and then it gives it back, too.

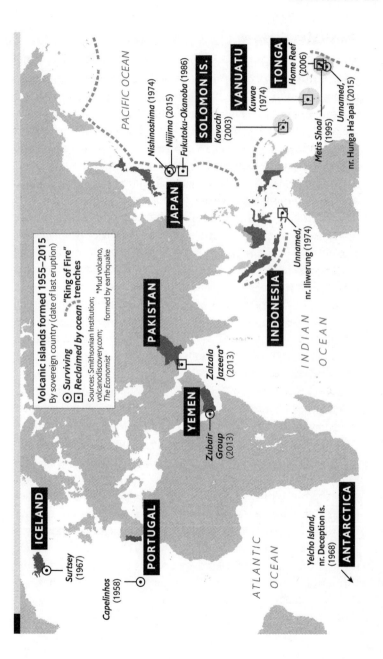

Volcanic islands formed 1955–2015
By sovereign country (date of last eruption)

⊙ Surviving   "Ring of Fire"
▣ Reclaimed by ocean ▬▬ trenches

Sources: Smithsonian Institution;
volcanodiscovery.com;   *Mud volcano,
The Economist   formed by earthquake

PACIFIC OCEAN

JAPAN
Nishinoshima (1974)
Niijima (2015)
Fukutoku-Okanoba (1986)

SOLOMON IS.
Kavachi (2003)

VANUATU
Kuwae (1974)

TONGA
Home Reef (2006)
Metis Shoal (1995)
Unnamed,
nr. Hunga Ha'apai (2015)

INDONESIA
Unnamed,
nr. Iliwerung (1974)

INDIAN OCEAN

PAKISTAN
Zalzala Jazeera* (2013)

YEMEN
Zubair Group (2013)

ICELAND
Surtsey (1967)

PORTUGAL
Capelinhos (1958)

ATLANTIC OCEAN

ANTARCTICA
Yelcho Island, nr. Deception Is. (1968)

How life on Earth began, probably

For most of the 20th century astronomers recognised just nine planets, including Earth. These days they know of more than 2,000, around the sun and other stars. But so far Earth remains unique in one important respect – it seems to be the only planet on which the strange, complicated mess of self-replicating chemistry called life has arisen. Faced with the awe-inspiring complexity of a living cell, the natural response is to wonder how such a thing could have begun in the first place. What do biologists reckon is the best explanation for the origins of life?

Modern cells rely on long strands of DNA to encode their genetic information, shorter strands of RNA to carry that information around; and proteins (made using that information) to run the chemical reactions they require to live. It is implausible that such a trifold system sprang into existence fully formed. However, one of its components, RNA, is able to carry out the functions of the two others, and may thus predate them. Like DNA, RNA can store genetic information, encoded in its structure. And like proteins, RNA can catalyse chemical reactions – including its own duplication.

Clues within modern cells suggest they may indeed be descended from purely RNA-based life. Almost all cells possess a structure called a ribosome, a molecular factory that strings proteins together from chemicals called amino acids. The structure of something so vital is likely to have been conserved, even over billions of years. And the business end of a ribosome, the part that actually does the assembling, is a single long strand of RNA. Modern cells also sport chemicals called ribozymes – enzymes made from RNA rather than from proteins – which perform various important cellular functions. Like the ribosome, they may be biochemical fossils from the earliest era of life. Such an "RNA world", in which small strands of the stuff copied themselves and sometimes mutated, may be theoretically plausible. But it raises another question: where did the RNA come from?

One way to answer that question is to start with some basic

chemistry and see what you can build. The most famous such experiment was performed in 1952 by Stanley Miller and Harold Urey. They filled a flask with water, hydrogen, ammonia and methane – a "primordial soup" of chemicals thought to be roughly representative of Earth's early atmosphere. Adding energy in the form of electrical sparks generated a sludge found to contain several types of amino acid. But that "primordial soup" theory has since fallen from favour. Scientists like Michael Russell, a researcher at NASA, argue instead that life may have started in underwater towers called "white smokers", built by volcanically heated, mineral-laden water bubbling up from beneath the ocean floor. Such smokers have a honeycomb structure, and experiments by Nick Lane of University College London show that the pores in this honeycomb could act as primitive cells, concentrating organic material inside themselves, and even setting up electrical gradients like those which power modern cells. Ultimately, in the absence of a time machine, it is only possible to argue about the relative plausibility of different theories. But the white-smoker theory for the origin of life is the most plausible one proposed so far.

Why salt may not be so bad for you after all

A traditional English breakfast features bacon, sausages and eggs – in other words, a whole lot of salt, or sodium chloride. But not, however, as much as it used to. A decade ago the government and health advocates began pressing companies to reduce salt levels in processed foods. As a result, in 2011 the English ate 15% less salt than in 2003. Researchers say this has led to improved cardiovascular health. Indeed, over the same period there was a 42% decline in deaths due to stroke and a 40% drop in deaths due to heart disease. The case against salt seems clear: people are healthier when they eat less of it. But some scientists remain sceptical. Why?

The more salt we eat, the more water our body retains. This increases blood pressure, at least until our kidneys flush out the salt and water. Those who see salt as a problem believe that the effect on blood pressure is more lasting, and that if too much salt is ingested over a long period of time it will cause hypertension and perhaps death. This would also explain why cutting down on salt reduces deaths from heart disease and strokes. A much-cited study carried out by America's National Institutes of Health in 2001, called the DASH-sodium study, found that participants put on diets that were lower in salt than the control group ended up with significantly lower blood pressure. This study forms the basis for many of the public-health pronouncements that demonise salt. America's dietary guidelines, based on "a strong body of evidence", put salt at the top of the list of things to avoid.

The body of evidence, though, is rather weaker than the American government lets on. The DASH study is one of many that have looked at the effects of salt intake on health. But others have failed to produce similar results. The 2003–11 analysis of salt consumption and health in England mentioned above found a correlation, but other factors – such as a simultaneous decline in smoking – seem more likely to account for the improved health outcomes. In 2011 two meta-analyses, which examine and combine the results from many different studies, were published by the

Cochrane Collaboration, a non-profit group that reviews medical evidence. The first found that reducing salt intake leads to lower blood pressure, but concluded that there is "insufficient evidence" that this leads to fewer premature deaths or a lower incidence of heart disease. The second concluded, quite simply, that "we do not know if low-salt diets improve or worsen health outcomes". The authors went on to say that "after more than 150 [randomised controlled trials] and 13 population studies without an obvious signal in favour of sodium reduction, another position could be to accept that such a signal may not exist".

Some researchers go a step further, claiming that reducing salt intake actually increases a person's risk of dying. The body needs some amount of sodium; if it gets too little the kidney secretes an enzyme called renin that can lead to hypertension. Some studies have found that low sodium levels are associated with increased risk of heart failure. Others suggest that a low sodium-to-potassium ratio may be the key to heart health. Much depends on the individual. The evidence is inconclusive, yet public-health officials have long presented the link between salt and heart disease as if it were fact. Such confidence is not warranted. There are plenty of reasons to avoid a full English breakfast, but salt may not be one of them.

Why there is weather in space

In March 2016, Britons enjoyed a rare treat: a display of the aurora borealis, better known as the Northern Lights, which could be seen as far south as Oxfordshire. That is unusual, for Britain is not all that boreal (northerly). Seekers after the Lights usually have to travel farther north to places like Scandinavia and Iceland to stand a good chance of seeing them. But the Lights are of interest to scientists as well as skywatchers, for they do not originate on Earth at all. They are caused by the interaction of the Earth's magnetic field with charged particles streaming from the sun, and are the most famous example of what is known as "space weather". That may seem a contradiction in terms: space is, famously, a pretty empty place. How is it possible to have weather there?

The reason is that space, particularly in the vicinity of stars and planets, is empty only by comparison with planetary surfaces. It has wind, in the form of the zillions of charged particles streaming from the sun. It has storms, in the shape of solar flares, enormous eruptions of plasma that spew charged particles out into space, and coronal mass ejections, which blast a quantity of the sun's mass out into the solar system. Stretch the metaphor a little, and space even possesses something a little like precipitation, in the form of clouds of dust and rock that we see from Earth as meteor showers.

For almost all of history, space weather was a mysterious, occasionally pretty irrelevance. But as mankind has become a space-faring species, scientists and engineers have had to take its effects more seriously. Solar flares can damage satellites and spacecraft, as happened to *Nozomi*, a Japanese Mars probe which was short-circuited by a solar flare in 2002. Astronauts aboard the International Space Station have special rooms in which to shelter from the high radiation levels caused by flares. But the effects are not always bad: in 2005, a particularly big solar flare actually caused radiation levels in the Earth's orbit to drop, as the magnetic fields generated by the cloud of ionised gas helped to deflect damaging cosmic rays from outside the solar system.

Space weather can also have effects on the ground. The charged particles that cause the aurorae emit radiation too. That is not a concern on the ground, where the thickness of the atmosphere offers adequate protection. But it is a worry at the sorts of altitudes at which modern airliners cruise. Trans-polar flights (such as those from Europe to America) can be diverted southwards if a big solar flare hits. The sun's tantrums can also disrupt the ionosphere, a charged layer in the atmosphere that can interfere with radio transmissions and the signals broadcast by GPS satellites. And in 1989 a geomagnetic storm (a disturbance in the Earth's magnetic field caused by a coronal mass ejection) induced big electrical currents in Quebec's electricity grid, cutting power to millions of people for nine hours. Space weather is less likely to disrupt your life than the terrestrial sort, but it is possible.

Why homeopathy is nonsense

Visit any health shop and you are likely to see them: packages of homeopathic remedies claiming to cure whatever ails you, from coughs and fever to insomnia and asthma. Flip the package of medicine, however, and you may be confused by the listed ingredients. Some claim to contain crushed bees, stinging nettles and even arsenic, as well as sugars such as lactose and sucrose. Americans alone spend some $3 billion a year on homeopathic medicines. What are they thinking?

The history of homeopathy – literally, "similar suffering" – dates back to the late 18th century. Samuel Hahnemann, a German doctor, was unimpressed by contemporary medicine, with good reason. Doctors used leeches to let blood and hot plasters to bring on blisters, which were then drained. In 1790, Hahnemann developed a fever that transformed his career. After swallowing powder from the bark of a cinchona tree, he saw his body temperature rise. Cinchona bark contains quinine, which was already known to treat malaria. Hahnemann considered the facts: cinchona seemed to give him a fever; fever is a symptom of malaria; and cinchona treats malaria. He then made an acrobatic leap of logic: medicines bring on the same symptoms in healthy people as they cure in sick ones. Find a substance that induces a symptom and it might be used to treat that symptom in another.

Hahnemann then decided that ingredients should be diluted and shaken repeatedly, a process called "potentiation". The smaller the amount of the active ingredient, the more powerful the medicine would become, he believed. Homeopathic remedies use various bits of terminology to convey their supposedly potency. One common designation is "NC", where C signifies that a substance is diluted by a ratio of 1:100 and N stands for the number of times the substance has been diluted. So a dilution of 200C would mean that one gram of a substance had been diluted within 100 grams of water, with the process repeated 200 times. At this dilution not a single molecule of the original substance remains when the water is used to make pills; most homeopathic pills thus consist entirely of sugar. However, the water and the pills are supposed to retain a "memory" of the original substance.

This is nonsense. Studying homeopathy is difficult, points out the world's biggest funder of medical research, the US National Institutes of Health (NIH), because it is hard to examine the effects of a medicine when that medicine has little or no active ingredient. Researchers can neither confirm that the medicine contains what it claims to nor show the chemical effect of the diluted medicine within the body. The most comprehensive review of homeopathy was published in 2005 in the renowned medical journal the *Lancet*. Researchers compared trials of homeopathic and conventional medicines. In the bigger, well-designed trials, there was "no convincing evidence" that homeopathy was more effective than a placebo, they found. Meanwhile, in similar trials of conventional drugs, medicines showed specific clinical effects. As the NIH drily notes: "several key concepts of homeopathy are inconsistent with fundamental concepts of chemistry and physics". That is putting it mildly.

Why there is a shortage of cadavers

Given that they are inert, smelly and upsetting to look at, it's a wonder that dead bodies are in such high demand. But for medical students they are an indispensable learning tool. In the 19th century, some medical schools hired bodysnatchers to dig up the deceased. William Harvey, the 17th-century English scientist who discovered the circulatory system, dissected his own father and sister. Today the procurement process is more civilised, but medical schools often complain about a lack of bodies. In the US there are regional shortages. In Asia and Africa the shortages are more acute. Some 60 million people die each year, so why is there a shortage of cadavers?

Growing demand is part of the problem. The number of medical students is increasing, as is the number of programmes that use cadavers. Certified doctors need bodies too, in order to continue their training. Researchers and pharmaceutical companies use bodies to develop new procedures and treatments. Organs also go to clinics and hospitals for transplants. Some bodies end up on display in exhibits after they are plastinated; others train police dogs to find disaster victims. A lucky few cadavers get to drive cars into walls in safety tests.

Supply, meanwhile, has not kept up. Improved means of communication mean there are fewer unclaimed bodies than there used to be in the past, which is one source of cadavers. Statistics on body donations – the other main source – are patchy, but such giving appears inconsistent and in many countries it is still taboo. In China and the Middle East, for example, dead bodies are treated with reverence, making their donation less common. Complicating matters is the fact that only certain bodies are suitable for medical study. A good cadaver is generally young, fully intact and not too obese or riddled with disease. It is perhaps not surprising that the supply of such bodies is limited.

Alternatives are being considered. High-tech mannequins, computer software and digital simulators are already used at some medical schools. But students say nothing beats the real thing.

One solution would be to pay for cadavers. In most countries with medical schools this is illegal, but there are still market forces at work. For example, schools will often pay for the cremation or burial of a body once it has served its scientific purpose. At least one study has shown a correlated increase in donations to those institutions. There is also a growing number of companies that match body donors with recipients. These firms are paid for services like removal, preservation and transportation of a body. Michel Anteby, a professor at Harvard Business School, calls it "a market for human cadavers in all but name".

What's behind the decline in bee populations?

Reports of bee die-offs have become more frequent and more alarming in recent years. Pollen from the world's flowering plants hitches a ride most often on bees, making them an integral part of the global food-production machinery. But distribution maps of which bees are where show contractions of range, and wholesale extinctions. There are widespread reports of vast die-offs in or sudden abandonments of honeybee hives, often called colony-collapse disorder. Bees are definitely dying – but why, and what might the consequences be?

The scope of what is at stake is sometimes misstated: around two-thirds of the food we eat, by weight, comes from staple crops such as rice, wheat and maize that are pollinated by wind, not insects. The remaining one-third includes fruits and vegetables, nuts, many herbs and spices, coffee and chocolate; a diet free of insect-pollinated foods would therefore be short on many nutrients and altogether pretty boring. Although bees are by far the biggest pollinators, a common misconception is that they are one uniform group. There are, in fact, about 20,000 bee species, but only a few are "honeybees" – that is, the kind that are kept in hives and are grown, sold and traded as a commodity no less than the crops they pollinate. The rest are wild. Though the balance of honeybee and wild-bee contributions varies widely, wild bees are responsible for a majority of pollination globally, and just a few species are doing most of this work (one study, published in *Nature* in 2015, estimated that 80% of pollination was accomplished by just 2% of bee species). So the decline of honeybees does not mean that all pollination by bees is at risk. That said, intensive farming of some crops such as almonds is entirely dependent on honeybees, because there are not enough wild bees to do the job in time reliably.

Intensive farming seems to underpin three distinct but interlinked challenges to bee populations. One is simple: worldwide, there is less uncultivated land available to support bees. Farmland is stripped of all but the cash-crop plants, so there is no flowery food when those crops are not in bloom. In many developed regions there is simply nowhere left for bees to roam. A second problem is the spread of honeybee diseases. Hives are shipped all over the world, and with them come stowaway bacteria, fungi and parasites such as the varroa mite, which has received much attention as a possible cause of colony-collapse disorder. Although they are associated with particular honeybee species, some of these nasties can jump the species barrier and threaten wild bees too. Third, intensive farming involves the use of a great many fungicides, herbicides and pesticides. In recent years a relatively new family of pesticides called neonicotinoids has drawn particular fire; while studies of the chemicals have had a confusing mix of results, it seems clear that at certain doses, and in combination with other, standard plant treatments, neonicotinoids can be harmful or even deadly to bees.

In all likelihood, the threat to bees is some complex interplay between these diverse stressors. Recent research, for example, has shown that tiny doses of the neonicotinoid clothianidin turns a largely harmless viral infection of European honeybees into a deadly one. Crop chemicals' effects on bees are typically studied one at a time, while the tremendous number of combinations to which bees are ultimately exposed go unexamined. And bee populations weakened by habitat loss or food shortage will, like any other creature, be more susceptible to additional threats. Returning some land to wild conditions is one simple fix; some schemes are already in place to reward farmers for doing so. Restricting the free passage of honeybee hives could help contain the spread of pathogens and parasites. But which combinations of problems are to blame in a particular hive or region, and whether any one cause ties together the losses worldwide, will remain a mystery until more studies can unpick this thorny interplay – no easy task when a majority of the critters concerned are free-roaming.

Noodles of longevity

China's economic rise is well-known. But the vast improvement in the health and longevity of its people – despite appalling levels of pollution – is less widely understood. A study published in the *Lancet* offers a province-by-province breakdown of China's health. Our map displays life expectancy at birth for each of the 33 provincial-level regions, matched with the country that is most similar by this measure.

The study shows that a baby born in China in 1990 would live on average to the age of 68. One born in 2013 could expect to reach 76. There is a large disparity between provinces, but the gap is narrowing. In Shanghai, life expectancy is now 83 – as good as Switzerland. People in six areas live longer than people in the US. The most impressive progress has taken place in the most benighted regions: a child in Tibet born in 1990 had a life expectancy of 56, akin to one of the poorest African countries. This has risen to 70, roughly the same as Moldova, one of Europe's poorer countries. The causes of death are also changing. There has been much progress in reducing infectious diseases (with the notable exception of HIV/AIDS). As in rich countries, diseases associated with lifestyle – such as strokes and heart disease – are now the biggest killers.

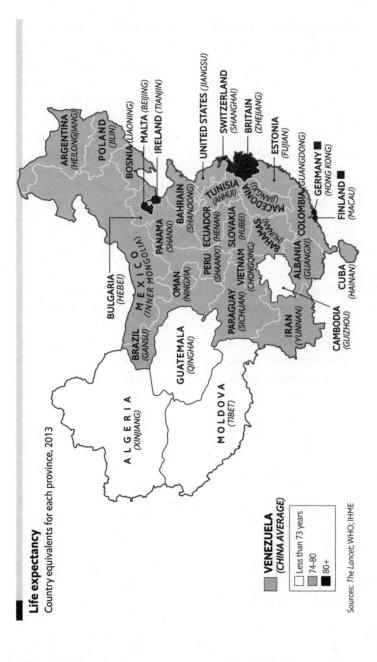

Life expectancy
Country equivalents for each province, 2013

□ Less than 73 years
▨ 74–80
■ 80+

Sources: *The Lancet*; WHO; IHME

How astronomers know "dark matter" exists

Astronomy is the most awe-inspiring of the sciences. To look up on a truly dark night, away from the light pollution of civilisation, is to be struck by the sheer amount of stuff that makes up creation. But modern astronomy teaches that the stuff that can be seen with the naked eye isn't even the half of it. The matter that can be seen spread across the sky as planets, comets, stars, nebulae, galaxies and the rest makes up just under 15% of the total. Astronomers have dubbed the remaining 85% "dark matter", because it neither absorbs nor gives off light. Although they are pretty sure it is real, they know nothing about it directly. How can scientists be so sure that something that is invisible is nevertheless there?

The simplest answer is that there seems to be too much gravity in the universe. The amount of matter that scientists can see through their telescopes is far too small to explain things like the structure of galaxies and the way in which stars within them move. In particular, galaxies appear to be spinning too fast to hold themselves together, at least judging by the amount of visible matter they contain. The gravitational attraction of unseen dark matter may be providing the necessary cosmic glue instead. One very close analogy is with the discovery of the planet Neptune in the 19th century. Neptune's existence was predicted before it was observed, when scientists noticed that the orbit of Uranus – Neptune's nearest neighbour – wasn't quite what Isaac Newton's theory of gravity said it should be. Mathematical analysis showed that assuming the existence of an unseen eighth planet in the solar system solved that problem nicely, and indeed such analysis led to Neptune's discovery. Similarly, assuming the existence of a large quantity of unseen extra mass neatly explains away the behaviour of the universe on very large scales.

There is another possibility, of course. If observations do not match theory, it might be because those observations are incomplete; or it might be that the observations are fine, but the theory is wrong. Perhaps gravity behaves differently, on very large scales, from the way that Einstein's theory of relativity predicts? Several astrophysicists have attempted to come up with tweaked theories of gravitation that could explain the movements of galaxies. The most famous, pioneered by Mordehai Milgrom in the 1980s, is called Modified Newtonian Dynamics, or MOND. But although MOND can explain some of what is seen, it struggles to explain everything. The majority of astrophysicists feel that the tweaks that MOND makes to the laws of gravity are messy and inelegant, and one of the wonders of physics is that elegance has, at least in the past, proved to be closely correlated with truth. And other observations buttress the idea that there is a lot of stuff out there that we simply can't see. One big one is the behaviour of the cosmic microwave background radiation – the faint afterglow of the Big Bang – which seems to be exactly as theory would predict, were dark matter real.

So almost all astronomers are convinced that a large helping of extra mass is called for. What exactly that mass is, though, is another question. Some of it may be quotidian – sunless planets, wandering black holes, old, cold stellar cores and the like. But the leading candidate is a new type of subatomic particle. Dubbed the wimp, for Weakly Interacting Massive Particle, this elusive beast is thought to interact with the universe via only gravity and the weak nuclear force, the feeblest pair of the four fundamental forces. As with the neutrino, which is similarly shy about making itself felt, that would make wimps very hard to detect. Many experiments have looked for direct evidence of their existence. So far, all have come up empty, which is an interesting result in itself. Each negative result shrinks the conceptual space in which wimps can be hiding. Most scientists expect a detection eventually. But if the searches were to continue to come up with nothing over the coming decades, that would be the most exciting result of all – because it would imply that we understand even less about the universe than we think we do.

Why Pluto is no longer a planet

In July 2015, *New Horizons*, a NASA space probe, completed its nine-year journey to Pluto. It arrived at a diminished world. When *New Horizons* was launched, on January 19th 2006, Pluto was the ninth and final planet from the sun; the only one never to have been visited by a robotic probe. Eight months later, on August 24th, the International Astronomical Union (IAU) voted to kick Pluto out of the planetary club. A generation of schoolchildren has thus grown up learning that the solar system has only eight planets, and that Pluto is, like astronomical also-rans such as Ceres, Eris and Makemake, merely one of the "dwarf planets". Why was Pluto demoted from the planetary club?

The immediate reason was that Pluto did not meet the definition of a planet that was formally agreed, for the first time, at the 2006 IAU meeting. To qualify as a planet, the astronomers decided, an object must be in orbit around the sun (so, for instance, Earth's moon does not count, despite being considerably bigger than Pluto). It must be massive enough to have become spherical under the force of its own gravity (which rules out things like asteroids and comets). And finally, it must have "cleared its orbit", either by absorbing other nearby objects into itself, or by kicking them out of the way with its gravity. That definition attempts to capture the intuition that planets should be the most notable features of solar systems after their stars. Pluto passes the first two tests, but fails the third. These days, it is clear that Pluto is merely one among thousands of "trans-Neptunian objects" (TNOs), itinerant hunks of rock and ice that drift around in the distant reaches of the solar system.

When Pluto was first discovered, in 1930, its claim to planethood seemed much stronger. At first, astronomers reckoned it was roughly as massive as Earth, based on calculations about how they presumed it was affecting the orbits of Uranus and Neptune. The estimate of Pluto's mass was then repeatedly revised downwards; first to around the mass of Mars, then (after measurements of

Pluto's reflectivity) to more like 1% of the mass of Earth. The discovery of Pluto's moon, Charon, allowed the estimate of its mass to be refined further. Today, the accepted value is about 0.2% of the mass of Earth. As Pluto's estimated mass fell, doubts grew about whether it should be counted as a full-blown planet. They became impossible to ignore in the mid-2000s, with the discovery of other, similarly sized objects beyond the orbit of Neptune. In 2005 a team led by Mike Brown, an astronomer at the California Institute of Technology, announced the discovery of Eris, another big TNO. Eris is almost as large as Pluto (with a diameter of 1,163km, compared with 1,184km for Pluto) and is about 25% more massive. If Pluto counted as a planet, there seemed no reason why Eris should not as well. And who knew how many more Eris-sized objects might lurk out in the darkness beyond Neptune? So the logical thing to do was to demote Pluto.

Some objected that this would require textbooks to be rewritten and would make wall-charts obsolete. But that is, in fact, a good thing. Pluto's reclassification is a very public demonstration of the way science works: when new evidence emerges that overturns what was previously accepted, the facts prevail, and the accepted theory is overthrown in favour of a new, more accurate understanding of the universe. And those with a sentimental attachment to Pluto who are still angry about the whole affair (and there are many, including some professional astronomers) may take some solace from the fact that this is not the first time in history that something like this has happened. When Ceres, the most massive of the asteroids (and now another member of the club of dwarf planets), was discovered, in 1801, it too was designated a full-blown planet. Only later, as it became clear that it was merely the largest constituent of a vast, messy disk of rocks orbiting between Mars and Jupiter – what is today called the asteroid belt – was its planetary status rescinded. So you could say that Pluto was kicked out of one very select club (the planets), only to join an even more select group: the club of astronomical bodies formerly known as planets.

Why the sky is blue

Summertime means the promise of cloudless blue skies, some of the time at least. What makes the sky this colour?

For scientists, the answer is relatively straightforward: Rayleigh scattering. When white light from the sun reaches the Earth, it hits the gas molecules that make up the atmosphere. These molecules – mainly nitrogen and oxygen – are smaller than the wavelengths of light in the visible spectrum, and so scatter the light. White light is made up of different wavelengths, which, since Isaac Newton's experiments with prisms in the 17th century, we think of as a spectrum of seven different colours: red, orange, yellow, green, blue, indigo and violet. Light at the violet end of the spectrum travels in shorter, tighter waves, which are affected more by the molecules in the atmosphere than the longer, lower-frequency waves at the red end. This phenomenon is named after Lord Rayleigh, the British physicist who discovered it in the 19th century. The sky appears blue because shorter wavelengths are scattered more by the atmosphere than longer wavelengths; so the scattered sunlight that reaches our eyes when looking at the sky (rather than at the sun itself) is predominantly blue.

But there is a catch: not everyone would agree that the sky is blue. In 1858 William Gladstone, better known for being the Prime Minister of Britain four times during the 19th century, published a treatise on Homer. He noted, with astonishment, that the Greek poet did not once use the word blue. He used colour words rather oddly – he described the sea as "wine-dark", iron as violet and honey as green. Further research showed that the Koran, the original Hebrew Bible, the Icelandic sagas and the Vedic hymns, written in India between 1500 BC and 1000 BC, also lack references to this hue, even when talking about the heavens. There are still many languages today that do not have a word that precisely correlates to the English word for the slice of the spectrum between green and purple. Russians might call the sky either *goluboe* (light blue) or *sinee* (darker blue); in Japan 青 (*ao*) encompasses the colour of the sky but also apples and grass; the Namibian Himba tribe would describe the sky as *zoozou*, which roughly translates as "dark" and includes shades of red, green and purple as well as blue.

This is more than a pedantic issue of translation: evidence suggests that language has a huge impact on how people interpret the world. Incredible as it may seem, having a distinct word for a colour reinforces and amplifies the perception of it as distinct from other shades. Without the word you don't perceive it as readily. To prove this, scientists showed groups of coloured tiles to the Himba, who found it difficult to pick out one blue tile from a group of 11 green ones (although they found it far easier than English-speakers to spot one yellow-green tile hiding amongst some more pine-hued ones). So although it is true that to English speakers the sky is blue, it is arguably blue only because they say it is.

How to make an invisibility cloak

Invisibility is a well-worn narrative device – one that has, you might say, made many appearances in fiction. Plato wondered if the mythical Ring of Gyges, which made its wearer disappear, would disturb a just man's morality as much as his visibility. A couple of millennia later, similar themes appeared in J. R. R. Tolkien's *The Lord of the Rings*. Just a few decades on from that, scientists conjured up transformation optics, a bit of mathematics that could skip the magic and promised to render objects invisible. The idea has now been inextricably linked to Harry Potter, a fictional boy wizard whose cloak lets him disappear, so that the scientific press abounds with examples of "invisibility cloaks". But how does a real-life invisibility cloak work?

To see an object is to detect the rail-straight rays of light that have impinged upon and bounced off it, and not to see any of the rays that come from the scene directly behind. To not see it, then, is to frustrate those processes: to prevent the scattering of light off the object, and to permit light from behind to pass unimpeded. A simple way to do this is to project or display on the front of an object an image of what is behind it – a technique known as "adaptive camouflage" that is being explored as a way to make tanks disappear from the battlefield. But the more captivating examples use metamaterials, man-made devices with structures and cavities comparable in size to the wavelength of light, which can be precisely engineered to carry out transformation-optics wizardry in a way that natural materials cannot.

The tiny structures within metamaterials can be used to bounce the light's constituent waves around, adding up here and cancelling out there in such a way that rays in effect curve around the cloak, and emerge travelling the same direction in which they had set out. Alternatively, metamaterial cloaks can be designed such that they precisely undo the light-scattering and absorption of the object they are hiding: taken together cloak and object look, to light and therefore to an observer, like empty space. To date, though, these approaches have only been made to work under lamentably limited conditions. The most compelling examples have been demonstrated in the microwave part of the electromagnetic spectrum, because it is easier to engineer structures at those longer wavelengths than at the much shorter ones of visible light. Cloaking demonstrations in the visible range could have hidden only the most diminutive of wizards. Prototypes are limited too in terms of the angle from which true invisibility can be claimed; seen from a different direction, a hidden object might be quite apparent. Most of all, though, cloaks are stiff, their shapes dictated by mathematics and their cloaking powers dependent on their shapes remaining unchanged.

A true Harry Potter cloak, then, remains a distant possibility. Luckily, the maths behind transformation optics can be applied elsewhere. Metamaterials are already being used to make more efficient radio antennas, for example. Other wave phenomena could benefit, too. Sound is just pressure waves, and smallish objects have been successfully cloaked in silence. Exploiting similar trickery could radically change concert-hall acoustics or headphone design. Earthquakes also create damaging waves; theoretical speculations on seismic cloaking have turned into a successful collaboration between scientists and civil engineers in France. They have shown that an array of empty boreholes around a large structure – a nuclear-power plant, say – might work as a shield from incoming seismic waves. Similar ideas put to work at sea might protect offshore platforms or even coastlines from tsunami waves. The potential benefits of understanding how to become invisible are plain to see.

Afterword: why explainer articles have become so popular

"WE ARE SEEKING A FIRST-CLASS EXPLAINER explainer to help readers make sense of the people who would make sense of the world for them... While most of your time will be spent creating explainer explainers, you will also occasionally round up other explainer explainers to create explainer explainer explainers." So ran a fake job ad on Medium, a blogging platform. Yet it is more than just a joke: the profession of "explainer" has exploded in recent years. Several upstart websites – Vox and FiveThirtyEight chief among them – are trying to build a business on the idea that things need to be explained. Established newspapers have followed suit: the *New York Times* has The Upshot; the *Wall Street Journal* answers questions such as "What is Alibaba?" and provides readers with "5 Things to Know" about important topics; and *The Economist* launched an explainer blog in 2013, from which much of the content in this book is derived. And then there is the mother of all explainer sites, Wikipedia, which boasts more than 31 million articles, each a primer on a different topic, in 287 languages. If you need to understand something in a hurry, reading the first sentence or two of a Wikipedia article is not a bad place to start. Why are explainers suddenly so popular?

The concept of the explainer as a journalistic form is not new. In a 2008 blog post, for instance, Jay Rosen, a journalism professor at New York University, argued that "there are some stories where until I grasp the whole I am unable to make sense of any part". Explainers should create "a scaffold of understanding that future reports can attach to," he argued.

The need for such a scaffold has always been there, says Professor Rosen today. But because newspapers used to be constrained by the amount of space available in print, this demand was mostly fulfilled with the hallowed "nut graf" – a paragraph that gives the outline and the context of the story in a nutshell. In the virtual realm there is unlimited space for explanation, and also much more of a need: readers are bombarded by ever more and ever smaller bits of information, which are hard to understand without knowing the background. In a way, explainers are a response to the endless streams of headlines, posts and tweets that are how most digital natives find their news today.

Explainers are therefore here to stay. A more difficult question is what form they should take. Wikipedia's entries start with a summary, but can then be very long and detailed. Vox's explainers are arranged instead as a collection of brief "cards". The articles in The Upshot read like in-depth analyses. *The Economist*'s explainers usually stick to a four-paragraph formula: set-up, background, explanation and implications. As always, there may be no best answer. In one of Rosen's classes, his students even wrote a song to enlighten listeners. Let a thousand explainers bloom.

Contributors

With many thanks to the following authors of the original *Economist* "explainers" and artists and data journalists who created the accompanying graphics:

James Astill, Ryan Avent, Hamish Birell, Sarah Birke, Emily Bobrow, Tamzin Booth, Jennifer Brown, Geoffrey Carr, Slavea Chankova, Bruce Clark, Tim Cross, Josie Delap, Graham Douglas, Doug Dowson, Richard Ensor, Gady Epstein, Jon Fasman, James Fransham, Lane Greene, Robert Guest, Loukia Gyftopoulou, Simon Hedlin, Evan Hensleigh, Emma Hogan, Charlotte Howard, Phil Kenny, Soumaya Keynes, Abhishek Kumar, Sarah Leo, Rachel Lloyd, Adam Meara, Dave McKelvey, Matt McLean, Roger McShane, Sacha Nauta, Andrew Palmer, Jason Palmer, John Parker, Lloyd Parker, Sophie Pedder, Charles Read, Bill Ridgers, Guy Scriven, Alex Selby-Boothroyd, Jane Shaw, Ludwig Siegele, Kassia St Clair, Stephanie Studer, Alexandra Suich, Alex Travelli, Tom Wainwright, Rosemarie Ward, Jonny Williams, Simon Wright, Yuan Yang, Wade Zhou.

For more "things you didn't know you didn't know" visit:
Economist.com/econexplains and Economist.com/graphicdetail

Index

The next big thing, before it's even a thing